Skipping Past Cornfields

Skipping Past Cornfields:

Musings from Mid-life

Juliana Davis Wallace

Contents

A Bit of Introspection

Maiden Voyage
(August 2010)

I swore that, despite my husband's gentle nagging, I would never cross the line and get my motorcycle license. Just not my cup of tea. Besides, my husband owns a Harley, and I found the roar annoying in a "look at me while I try to impress you with my manliness" kind of way.

And yet, just the other day, I found myself revving the engine of the Harley at a stoplight, enjoying the feeling of power beneath me and chuckling gleefully at the fact that in just a few minutes I would destroy the peace and quiet of my suburban neighborhood. Nearly a year with an M on my license. Yes, taking that motorcycle safety class was the most intimidating thing I have ever done. But I have to say, life looks better from the back of a bike.

In the spirit of crossing lines I never thought I would cross, I begin a blog. Chalk it up to midlife crisis and a persistent need to prod myself into accomplishing a goal or two. I have always considered blogging an exercise in egocentric exhibitionism. I mean, really, who honestly cares about the inner workings of the average mind? Well, probably no one. But at this point, the need to exercise my brain supersedes my caring what anyone thinks. So off I go. Cornfields to my right, soybeans to my left, I skip into the sunset.

Of Skunks, Toilets and Flight
(August 2010)

I tucked my daughter into bed just now. Per our usual routine, I gave the preamble prayer. "Please help Kristina and Jared (don't forget Jared, Mom) not to have any bad dreams, and please help Kristina not to dream about smelling any skunks." I am not sure that Kristina would know a skunk if she smelled one, but she has me say the same prayer every night, nonetheless.

My husband tells me his dreams in detail when he wakes up. Somehow, verbalizing and examining that bridge into his day puts things into their proper places, like shutting drawers or making the bed. I, on the other hand, rarely remember my dreams. When I do remember them, I find they generally fall neatly into one of the categories in a dream analysis book. For instance, I was relieved to discover that other normal women also, apparently, spend their sleeping hours wandering past filthy bathroom stalls in vain search for a relatively clean and private place to relieve themselves. Who knew?

In my favorite dreams I fly. Sometimes I soar almost effortlessly. At other times I tire with the labor of flapping my arms to stay aloft. Even when my arms ache, however, I marvel at the fact of my flight.

I have missed those flying dreams in recent years. Though happy enough, I have let my lack of ambition and the weight of everyday routine ground me. Garden variety escape dreams litter my early morning sleep now, dreams that wither quickly in the post-waking reality. I miss the view from above, the power of flight in my arms, and the faith in the impossible.

Just in the past few days, with a couple of simple goals to spur me on, I have begun to feel a tingle of possibility again. Time to dust off those dreams, flex my flying muscles, and reacquaint myself with the world above. Sweet dreams!

Solitude

(October 2010)

I have discovered that, in addition to the usual life-sustaining necessities, there are a few items critical to my well-being. When these fall out of balance, I become edgy, unsettled. I need regular spiritual study and daily exercise. I need to write. And I need time alone. I suppose I also require social contact, but as I cannot currently seem to escape people these days, I have not felt sufficient lack of society lately to recognize any conscious craving for it. Due to circumstances beyond my control, I have missed my coveted hours of solitude this week. The loss has set me to fantasizing about how I would spend a couple of hours alone with my own thoughts. In true David Letterman fashion, I will post my top 10 list.

Number 10: Lock the door, turn up the music (something rather loud, with a decent beat), and clean. Then, with the dust and grime a not so distant memory, relax into the sofa, smell the subtle hint of Pine Sol, and soak in a fleeting moment of order and calm.

Number 9: Dine alone in a restaurant, preferably one with a garden view, an artsy decor, and enough of a crowd so that I can observe the other patrons anonymously and imagine their back stories. Order something light, with an exquisite blend of flavors. Wash it down with sparkling water and a twist of lime and tie it all up with dark chocolate and herb tea.

Number 8: Don leather and hop on the Harley for a motorcycle ride through the countryside. Watch the sunlight sparkle on the lake as I pass.

Number 7: Close the blinds, turn down the lights, locate a CD of rain song, and meditate. Find ohm.

Number 6: Watch a movie, perhaps something on the order of Jane Austen or *Room with a View*. It must be entertaining and can even verge on frivolous, but it must also be well done.

Number 5: Go for a hike. The Sunset Ridge trail on Mount Mansfield fits the bill as well as anything else. It starts in the trees, shaded and intimate, but soon opens up to an expansive view and culminates above the tree line, overlooking mile upon mile of humanity, softened by hazy afternoon sunlight and too far away to be obtrusive.

Number 4: Settle into a steaming hot bath, with scented candles and soft music.

Number 3: Visit an art museum. Rush through the ancient history and cubism exhibits. Slow down as I round the corner to the Impressionists. Drink in the likes of Monet and Van Gogh, then move on to Edward Hopper, Frank Lloyd Wright, and Ansel Adams. Breathe until my soul fills to the brim with beauty.

Number 2: Write. The result will fall short of the great American novel, perhaps, but ideally it will involve something profound, not so grand as to inspire nations but rather so true that it introduces the reader to his or her own soul.

Number 1: Gather my herb tea and a book, arrange the pillows just so, and settle back on the bed to read. Fight to keep my eyes open just long enough to allow the urge to grow impossible to resist. Then let my book fall to the side and surrender to sleep, a mug of vanilla chamomile cooling at my elbow.

Bliss List

(November 2010)

Last year for Christmas, our friends gifted us a subscription to *Cook's Illustrated* magazine. I like the recipes just fine, and the cooking tips are marvelous. If I renew my subscription, however, it will be for the superb editorials by Christopher Kimball, a fellow Vermonter. When the first issue arrived on my doorstep, I opened it to find Kimball's "Bliss List." In the essay, he describes several of the handful of moments of absolute and perfect happiness that he has experienced in his life. That got me to thinking about some of my own blissful moments. I'll include just a couple of those here.

- I am spinning on a hilltop, arms stretched wide in my own imitation of Maria in the opening scenes of *The Sound of Music*. I even sing and laugh out loud, because no one can hear me. With each step I bounce a bit on springy, fragrant tundra. The wind carries my laughter away and blows the hair back from my face. As I spin, I see nothing to suggest human presence–just tundra, mountains, wind and clouds. I know that a short hike down the hill and around the bend will bring me in sight of a float plane and a handful of businessmen playing out their Alaskan fishing adventure. But high above the stream I can neither see the blue of the plane nor hear the occasional voice. For the moment, this corner of the wilderness exists only for me.

- It is early in the year 1978, with South Dakota in the midst of a historic winter. I open my eyes to see nothing but white outside my window. Tugging the blue quilt close around my neck, I wiggle my toes and listen. The wind rattles the window next to my bed, and the branches of the mulberry tree scratch the glass. In the middle of the night the sound would leave me paralyzed with fear, but on a weekday morning it sends a hopeful smile spreading across my face. My mother listens to the radio in the kitchen as she makes breakfast. Over the clatter of plates and pans I hear the announcer begin the school closings. Thankfully, Mother turns up the radio. Near the end of a long list I hear "Yankton Public Schools closed." No school today! I wait for the call to breakfast and gaze at the snowflakes while I contemplate a day of snowdrifts and hot cocoa.

- It is the spring of my first year of college. I sit on the back of a motorcycle, flying along a back road in southern Idaho. Mark and I chat occasionally on our helmet mics, but mostly we just take in the scene around us. By the time we make it back to Logan, we will probably miss our next class, but today the early spring sunshine in the Rockies seems more important than French verbs or World History. We pass small farms, cows lazily munching new grass, and a large abandoned barn that makes me dream of swinging into bales of hay even though I have only read about it and never actually done it. Ours is an easy friendship, comfortable and without the pressure of romance. Mark stands a little apart from the boys I date—neither the straight-laced Mormon that his Merrill heritage would suggest, nor a self-proclaimed rebel, either. He challenges my comfort zone with this motorcycle, and I like that. I lean against the backrest, warm with friendship and the sun on my shoulders.

Bonding Moments

(December 2010)

I reacted rather strongly to a blog entry recently, a reaction that has set me pondering about blogging in general, the peculiarities of how women relate to one another, and the benefits and follies of communal grieving. I am relatively new to blog world, and I have explored little of that world so far. I love eavesdropping on my nephew's rather remarkable thought processes, and peaking over the fence into my friend's gardening adventures has made me long for the Pacific Northwest and a green thumb.

My experiences with a group blog written by and for women have been more mixed. The accomplished writers on this blog deliver polished, engaging material for the most part. With vivid images and fluid prose, they draw their readers close to the heart. From the comments I have read, it is clear that the essays on the blog resonate with their audience. Still, I have this growing sense that as I read I am peering in on an ongoing group therapy session. Nearly every entry details a death, a troubling diagnosis, a heart-wrenching case of abuse, the daily struggles of motherhood, or a series of slights from a group of people who "should know better."

The recent entry that sparked my reaction was a case in point. The writer spoke eloquently of her grieving process following a tragic loss. I ignored the "group therapy" thought tickling the back of my mind as I followed along. In fact, I managed to keep the silly inner voice at bay right up until the blogger began to lament the fact that the only person who seemed to "get" her grief and know what to say was a perfect stranger. Others gave her the silent treatment, and she resented it, particularly at church where her fellow worshippers should know how to mourn with those that mourn.

My pesky inner voice began to grow louder. By the time I glanced through a couple of the dozens of commiserative comments, I gave the voice free rein and quickly turned away from the computer before I could surrender to the temptation to add a comment of my own. I have no problem with the very real pain of loss, just with making others responsible for sharing that pain gracefully.

What is it that bothers me so much about this poignant essay and so many others like it? After all, I get plenty of blog mileage out of my own inner turmoil. I think there are a few primary ingredients to my frustration. I do not understand why women, in particular, seem to have a penchant for bonding over tragedies. It is as if someone created a special club. To gain entrance into the club, or at least to earn the privilege of offering an opinion, one must present her tragedy at the door. Fine. I'll pay up. The things that truly stab me in the gut these days I prefer not to discuss publicly, but I think losing a spouse should be enough to give me a turn at the mic.

I do claim a rudimentary understanding of the grieving process, enough to realize that the process has as many flavors as there are mourners. I also realize that just as we have a responsibility to help shoulder each other's burdens, we also need to take final responsibility for dealing with our own pain. Yes, it would be wonderful if everyone knew just what to say to the survivor of a loss or the single mother struggling for a finger hold. Occasionally, someone will, indeed, strike a profound chord--by inspiration or accident, or simply by virtue of the sufferer's own readiness to accept the

Savior's comfort. More often, spectators to grief or pain offer silence or awkward, even hurtful, attempts at conversation. Most folks find the spectre of another's grief incredibly intimidating. We ache for the wounded heart behind the brave face or the tears, and in our fear of miss-step we too often turn away. Grief is such a personal matter, and sometimes we turn aside to give the sufferer a chance to throw a robe around the naked pain. I do not condone the silence, but I do understand it.

Just now, I read through portions of my journal from the cancer years. I marveled again at the heroism of neighbors and co-workers, family and church members who heeded inspiration and bravely entered the foreign world of my pain. I also remember a dark afternoon when I pleaded in prayer for relief from a burden I felt was too heavy to bear. The Lord answered my prayer with a phone call from my great aunt. Aunt Fae had walked in my shoes, nursed a husband who died from a similar illness, and I just knew she would say something wonderful to ease the burden. I kept no record of the details of our conversation, but I vividly remember that it did not offer the healing balm for which I had hoped. Instead, it gave me something I needed more that afternoon: a pair of emotional hiking boots and a prod up the trail. I miss my Aunt Fae.

And the Not So Blissful Moments

(February 2011)

I remember the exact point at which I stopped watching the movie *Schindler's List*. By all accounts, the movie is a masterpiece and the story gripping, but I could not watch it. I have a vague memory, perhaps faulty, of a scene of soldiers moving through the ghetto, spreading violence and fear in their path. Desperate for her child's life, a mother tosses her baby out a window...to a waiting soldier who impales the infant on the point of his bayonet. Whenever I need to feel my insides curl into a tight little ball, I remember that scene.

Some time ago, I wrote about bliss moments, scenes etched in my memory because they evoke warm and cozy feelings. I hold quite a store of bliss moments. In another corner of my brain, etched just as powerfully, I have a store of anti-bliss moments, memories of times that stopped a smile dead in its tracks. This set of memories occupies a much smaller and less accessible portion of my psyche, and yet I hold on to these ragged images, feeling somehow that they, too, have something to offer me.

Oddly, outside of movies or novels, scenes of death and classic tragedy rarely figure on my anti-bliss list. Instead, my unhappy moments often tend toward the much more prosaic--flashing lights in my rear view mirror, for instance. In fact, just last week I had to dig into the bottom of my purse and smooth out a badly crumpled traffic ticket before sending it to the court clerk. I confess that I behaved rather badly when the conscientious police officer delivered the ticket, and I let loose a torrent of tears and objectionable vocabulary once he had moved on to his next victim. For days, I could not even talk about the ticket, responding in stony silence to my family's teasing.

Even now, my calm restored, I cannot quite articulate why a simple traffic stop sparked such an intense response. I think perhaps my overactive need for perfection balks at such a blatant reminder of my too human nature.

A rather prominent shelf in my anti-bliss storage closet holds memories of interpersonal conflict, not because I court contention but because those moments bother me more than almost anything else. On the simple end are moments such as the time I unwittingly cut off another driver headed for the same parking spot. Furious, the other driver flashed the international sign of contempt and yelled something rather unintelligible. In my surprise and hurt (I was 20, mind you, and rather naive) I attempted to respond in like manner, but I was shaking too badly to figure out which finger should point to the blue skies above. The incident bothered me for hours, which strikes me now as quite silly. Years later, I discovered that responding with a smile and a wave has the advantage of both disarming my opponent and reducing my own blood pressure quite handily. Beautiful discovery, that.

Less humorous and more striking are those times when discord settles on my doorstep, when misunderstandings wedge their way between me and one of those persons I love most dearly. When contention comes home, when I perceive a threat to bonds I hold eternal and lack the power or knowledge required to sew up the wound, those are the times I long to inflict on myself some sort of pain to distract me from hurt I cannot either understand or control. Fortunately, those moments occur rarely, and I have learned better how to cope when they do slide under the door.

Happily, I can bring forward few memories that travel beyond the mundane and almost no lingering angst from feeling offended. Whether I lead a charmed life, or whether my naïveté simply leaves me blind to offenses, I could not say. I do find it intriguing that I seem to fear conflict, embarrassment, and loss of control above just about anything else.

I hope I never have the opportunity to feel the desperation of the Jewish mother in *Schindler's List*. I hope that I have taught my children to learn from their struggles and to store up blissful moments to give them strength in the darkness. And I hope that my own memory of pain will help me to grow in beautiful ways.

Power in Weakness

(February 2011)

My husband, bless his heart, knows me entirely too well. Despite all his protestations to the contrary, I remain convinced that he occasionally exploits that understanding for his own wicked amusement. Take basketball, for instance. I like to watch basketball occasionally, love the grace and strength, the dazzle of a well-played game. And yes, for all of you fellow Celtics fans, Rajon Rondo is a beautiful man.

I do not, however, play basketball. If I have any grace and strength, those qualities flee when I take a basketball in my hands. Team sports and I never quite connected in a meaningful way. After nearly two decades of marriage, my husband should know this. And yet...a few weeks ago, I opened my email to find the unwelcome announcement from my son's basketball coach that he had scheduled a mother/son basketball game. Did I neglect to mention that my husband coaches my son's team?

For two weeks, I dreaded that game. I pouted, whined and tried to weasel out, but the night of the big game found me glowering in the car on the way to the gym. Far outside my comfort zone, smack in my weak spot, this game held little promise of the great fun my husband gleefully anticipated.

To my credit, I left my pouting courtside and threw myself into the game. I even made a couple of baskets, although I avoided dribbling at all costs. We had a grand time, and I was laughing too hard to slap the smug grin off my husband's face. Drat that man!

In the days leading up the game, I contemplated my aversion to my own weaknesses. I love feeling strong, physically and emotionally. I love to succeed, to work my way to the top of the mountain and breathe in the view. And yet, that annoying voice inside me, the voice that sounds rather like my husband, reminded me of the power of weakness.

Paul, the little apostle of immense courage who stood boldly before kings, proclaimed, "When I am weak, then am I strong." He recognized that the strength of the Lord was made perfect in the weakness of His servants. This same God wrapped His greatest treasure, His most potent force, in the body of a tiny baby and sent that baby to the home of a lowly carpenter. This same God, Paul wrote to the Corinthians, "hath chosen the weak things of the world to confound the things which are mighty."

I have not yet reached the point where I readily, like Paul, glory in my weaknesses. But I confess to a fascination with the concept of weakness as power. Ether, the *Book of Mormon* prophet, quotes the Lord in what is, to me, one of the most hopeful verses in all of scripture: "And if men come unto me I will show unto them their weakness. I give unto men weakness that they may be humble; and my grace is sufficient for all men that humble themselves before me; for if they humble themselves before me, and have faith in me, then will I make weak things become strong unto them." (Ether 12:27)

The strength that I admire, the strength of Paul and Peter and all the truly great men and women, comes only when we acknowledge our weaknesses in humility and exercise the faith necessary to allow the Lord to transform them. God is, after all, the master alchemist. Who am I to let a little fear of failure stand in the way of the treasure God could make of my life? Let's play ball!

Answer to the Hard Question, Take Two
(September 2011)

I began writing this blog just over one year ago, partly to exercise my writing muscles and partly to answer what was, for me, a challenging question. After a youth and young adulthood spent building a résumé of accomplishments and adventures, I found myself in middle age with increasingly blurred vision. Not only did I require glasses to read anything smaller than about 18 point type, but I had lost sight of myself. When faced with a seemingly innocuous request to describe myself, I froze.

Last week, I asked my early morning seminary students to respond to the question: Who am I? I decided that I should answer the question myself, and for the first time in several years, I found the task surprisingly easy. In no particular order:

I am a writer, or at least I aspire to be a writer. For years, I brought in a pretty good salary writing manuals and proposals, and yet I did not consider myself a writer. Now, my pen brings in absolutely no income at all. All the same, my brain needs to write almost as much as my body needs to eat. I love it when my writing touches someone else, but I would write even without an audience.

I am a teacher. This year, that involves teaching music and scriptures, but frankly, I enjoy teaching just about anything. Sometimes I think I have a talent for teaching. On my better days, I realize my flaws and focus on learning and listening and letting something greater than I do the teaching. That works much better. I do draw the line at opening a preschool or teaching computer skills to octogenarians. We all have our limits, unreasonable as they may be.

I am a wife and a mother, and I say that with much more meaning now than I did in my twenties when I first took the titles. Life and death, epiphanies in the pit or on the mountaintop, and the plodding pace of daily life have all led me step by step to a much greater understanding of what it means to be married and live in a family.

I am a believer. I have had occasion these past few months to revisit and refresh my beliefs. After an unexpected period of doubt, I pondered back over my own personal experiences with God and with the Church of Jesus Christ of Latter-Day Saints. I cannot explain the experiences of others or events that occurred years ago. On the other hand, neither can I deny the unmistakable answers to prayers, the inspired counsel of leaders, and the direct influence of God in my life and the life of my family. I know God lives and that He communicates not only with me but with His prophet on the earth. Call it simple if you will. I cannot deny what experience has taught me to be true.

How refreshing to discover myself again! I have missed me.

Perfection, Proportion and Other Myths

(November 2011)

I have always aspired to an exalted vision of the "strong, silent type." You know the character: soft-spoken yet profound, mild but still commanding reverence, polished. If I were true to that vision, I would discipline my children gently, yet firmly and with complete consistency. Better yet, I would set such a sterling example and inspire such devotion that they would rarely feel the need to whine or misbehave.

I would have no occasion to cringe at the memory of long ago dating mishaps, never having fallen into the cliché of a rebound relationship or a regretted kiss. Memory would find no emails sent or words spoken in the heat of frustration with inadequate information. I would care less about politics and more about anonymously doing good. And at my funeral, in some distant future, my children would brag about how their mother never raised her voice or engaged in creative profanity, how she never left a project unfinished. In short, they would paint a picture of the perfect lady, and everyone would pause to wipe a tear and sigh at the memory.

Sadly, I will never reach the lofty heights of that perfect woman perched rather uncomfortably--but with such grace--on her pedestal. I will continue to blurt out rough-cut sentiments, only to immediately wish the words back safely in my head. I will periodically set off on grand quests, turning around in short order once reality sets in. I will care too much or not enough. I will respond too quickly and too passionately to the opinions of total strangers.

Back in my college days, a friend said something to the effect that anything worth it was bound to get a little messy along the way. In the midst of our often muddled love lives and the fallout of all the cumbersome life decisions that faced us as young adults, we clung to that philosophy. With all the messiness in our lives, it was comforting to envision grandeur on the horizon.

Recently, while reading E.M. Forster's *Howard's End*, I discovered the Schlegel family. Admittedly, this novel fell rather lower on my favorites list than I expected. Still, the inner life of the characters left me with much to ponder. Margaret Schlegel, speaks of "proportion," a notion that captures some of the sense of balance and grace that I envision in that ideal woman on the pedestal. While acknowledging the worthy goal of living a perfectly balanced life, Margaret cautions, "Don't begin with proportion. Only prigs do that. ... though proportion is the final secret, to espouse it at the outset is to ensure sterility."

I try to stay on the fringe of the political scene, having come to the realization that my active participation in the process only leads me to frustration and belligerence. However, I follow the elections enough to notice a tendency toward sterility. We criticize one candidate for her clothes, another for his morals, and another for speaking off script. Candidates for high office, it seems, need to burst onto the scene with proportion well in hand or suffer defeat.

Years ago, a young lawyer ran for president. He was tall, gaunt, plagued with debilitating depression, occasionally suicidal. In today's media scene, Abraham Lincoln's political liabilities would likely push him out of the running in short order. Yet, according to Joshua Wolf Shenk, in the article "Lincoln's Great Depression," "With Lincoln we have a man whose depression spurred him, painfully, to examine the core of his soul; whose hard work to stay alive helped him develop crucial skills and capacities, even as his depression lingered hauntingly; and whose inimitable character took great strength from the piercing insights of depression, the creative responses to it, and a spirit of humble determination forged over decades of deep suffering and earnest longing."

Like many of us, Lincoln lived an untidy life. The national chaos in which he lived formed a backdrop for the inner debris of a lack of formal education and a profound melancholy. Lincoln's constant struggle to achieve balance formed his character in critical ways, giving him the skills he needed to lead the nation at a pivotal moment. Proportion without struggle would have left him handicapped.

I hold on to that goal of balance, or proportion, and I periodically achieve it for a time. It gives shape to my wanderings and invites beauty and peace. In turn, the wanderings, with all of their occasional messiness, lend dynamic tension to the plateaus of balance. Lacking the wanderings, we would have tidiness without substance, order without elegance.

All in a Day's Work

(January 2012)

I have spent the last few days working retail for minimum wage. At the mall, no less. Yes, the mall. That place I avoid like the plague. That hallmark of American capitalism scented with the ubiquitous odor of Abercrombie meets Yankee Candle meets Cinnabon. I hate to shop, and my days of stalking the cute boy in the music store have long past. Besides, malls remind me of so much of what I deplore in society: shelves stuffed with useless merchandise simply to provide the illusion of prosperity and give us the opportunity to make pointless choices, teenagers wasting time when the world offers so much more than they realize they can attain, food designed to plunge us further into the pit of obesity.

And yet...this has been a good week. Let's face it. A temporary job came when I needed the money. Until I figure out the magic formula for earning my living by my pen or land an interesting job that allows me to wrap my arms around my daughter when she skips down the school bus steps in the afternoon, the local economy offers me limited options. Besides, this retail job affords me time with a dear friend and coworker, and if it interrupts my usual exercise routine, at least the hours of loading boxes on a trailer keeps the muscles from atrophy.

I have had ample opportunity while counting inventory and loading boxes to ponder the difference in my life now from when I last worked for someone else over a decade ago. I note with some sense of surprise how guilty I feel about my soft life. I often deplore the lack of sufficient hours in the day. And yet, I find time to exercise for an hour or two every day. I nap occasionally (although, since I wake up each morning at 5 a.m. to teach a class, I feel less guilty about that). I spend hours at the computer researching and writing a book that I will never sell. Occasionally, not often enough, I snag an hour or two to read a novel. I never watch TV.

This week, when I come home from work wanting a chance to unwind and simply get off my feet for an hour, I hesitate before complaining to my husband, realizing more now than last month just how much he sacrifices his own time for the family. I remember how much I used to accomplish when I worked a demanding job and traveled frequently, yet still managed to teach early morning seminary and raise children and make dinner on a fairly regular basis. I fear my capacity to achieve has diminished.

I remind myself that Brad played the supporting role when I lived a corporate life, making my full schedule a possibility. I think of the stress that full schedule caused and the peace that gradually set in when I traded the day planner for a more sedate life at home. I see the value in developing my creative side and providing an anchor for the family. Still, as I finish up my week as a mall rat, I tender a moment of gratitude for the reminder of the rare blessing it has been to raise my children and find myself over these past 13 years. I renew my appreciation for my husband. And I savor more than ever a "soft" life that may not last much longer.

A Rebellion in Bloom

(June 2012)

The sky threatened rain this morning, or rather promised it, and the wind covered the grass underneath the plum trees with rose petals. It all sounds lovely and romantic, with a scented carpet of yellow and pink. From the road, it looks as if the yellow rosebush fairly exploded with color, spilling sunshine. A closer inspection, however, reveals leaves spotted with holes and blooms past their prime. My rosebushes needed a haircut before the approaching rain left them looking like street beggars in faded rags once vibrant.

Accordingly, I put the dog out on her chain for her morning sniff and forage and gathered my clippers from the tool chest. Much to the consternation of Emily Post or the mothers of random southern debutantes or whoever really cares about such things, I padded around to the flower garden in my pajamas to gather spent blooms and attempt to tidy up my rather messy garden.

I know little about gardening, from the perspective of either aesthetics or horticulture. The first year in our new home, the day lilies timidly hugged the side of the garage, leaving plenty of space for rosebushes and a small, unassuming black-eyed Susan plant. But the day lilies have now thrown away any pretense at timidity, flinging their skinny green arms wide and boldly claiming new territory. From a distance I fail to distinguish the yellow lilies from the roses they overshadow. Not content with their own debauchery, the lilies have corrupted the black-eyed Susans and they, too, have willfully chosen to ignore their boundaries.

Amid the rebellion of the garden stand four rose bushes: one staunchly white, one sunny yellow, one white edged in pink, and one that blooms pink and fades to lavender. The roses love sunshine and heat. When I wilt in the 90 degree weather, they burst forth in an untidy profusion of dozens of blooms. I cut a bouquet of garden flowers over the weekend, arranging them in a vase on the dining room table. Away from the blue sky and fresh air, however, the blooms paled sadly and drooped a bit, no longer confident in the absence of sunshine.

I grew up with roses on the south side of the house. Mother tested new roses for Jackson and Perkins in those days, flowers with names like Snowfire and Yankee Doodle. I remember the white boxes arriving in the mail and scrawny bushes soaking in the bathtub before Mother planted them in her garden alongside the driveway. She planted hybrid teas, mostly, elegant flowers that would never explode willy-nilly in quite the way mine do. Roses like the ones in my childhood memories belong in orderly gardens, well-spaced and well-tended.

My roses have neither the beauty of the hybrid teas, nor the freedom of the day lilies. Their blooms lack polish and proper balance. They fail to present as well in a vase as they do out in the sunshine. At the same time, try as they will, they cannot reach thorny branches as wide as they would like. I trim the bushes a little each time I cut a drooping bloom, and I cut them back to almost nothing in the winter, leaving naked stumps to weather out the frost and snow.

I have been thinking lately about gardens, about living somewhere in the nether zone between elegance and freedom. I remember a few hybrid tea days, when my résumé brimmed with promise. But the days I miss are the lily days, those years when I flung my arms wide and thoroughly enjoyed life. I traveled. I explored intellectual landscapes and watched the world open up before me. I recognized only those boundaries I chose to accept.

I no longer feel the freedom of the lily days. The modesty of my bank account, combined with the responsibilities that tend to accompany middle age, keep that kind of freedom tantalizingly out of range. Cornfields out my kitchen window lack the breathtaking quality of Alaskan summers or the wonder of a full moon through the steam of a geyser.

And yet, maybe the simple lilies still have lessons to teach me. They create free space between the garage and the bricks, ignoring artificial boundaries, thriving in the heat and soaking up the rain. They even handle the occasional frost, cheerfully rebounding with blossom after blossom. I think maybe I can find some lily days again. I just have to remember how to stretch my arms and twirl.

Soul Food

(October 2012)

Recently, a friend and I chatted about ballroom dancing. My friend is a lovely woman, with a classic and timeless beauty. I watched her dance once, and even while dancing with an amateur partner, she exuded a captivating grace. To me, ballroom dance represents the epitome of elegance: Audrey Hepburn in motion, if you will.

I asked my friend to tell me her favorite dances. The first answer came easily and seemed a natural fit. For smooth dance, she loves the flowing elegance of the waltz. She hesitated a bit on her choice of a favorite rhythm dance. "I used to hate the cha-cha-cha," she said. "The movement is different, and I've had to work very hard at that dance." She went on to describe her early discomfort with the dance, the syncopated hip movements and the sensuality that challenged her and dragged her far from her comfort zone. But she has grown to love the form, and I sense that she has discovered much about herself in the process, a self awareness that has nothing and everything to do with dance. Our food came and the conversation turned to other topics, but I have reflected on our chat and how dance fits into my own musings of late.

Yesterday, needing to ponder through my conundrum of the week, I threw on sneakers and left my quiet house just after dawn, needing the movement of a brisk walk in the wind to set my thoughts in motion and help me sort through them. For a while, I just let the wind move through my head as I felt the rhythm of my footfalls and let my mind wander. After a time, the thoughts began to arrange themselves into patterns.

I have been examining some of my own prejudices and reactions lately. Many of us at times seek to deny the physical appetites in order to enhance the spiritual. For example, Hindu monks eat only to sustain life. Catholic priests and many Buddhist monks take a vow of celibacy. Even in mainstream society we periodically fast for greater religious insight, subjugating the physical. We read scriptures like Matthew 26:41, which says, "the spirit indeed is willing, but the flesh is weak" and we come to the seemingly logical conclusion that the spirit is superior to the body. For me, that occasionally evolves into the error of associating things primarily physical with weakness.

My light bulb moment for the morning walk started with a scripture. Doctrine & Covenants 88:15 reads, "And the spirit and the body are the soul of man." The soul, the post-resurrection self on the path to perfection, is comprised not of the spirit alone, but of the spirit and the body. We bury the spirit in baptism and the body in death. Through the Savior's atonement, both spirit and body rise again, joined inseparably.

I thought back to the cha-cha-cha and other similar journeys of self-discovery that blend the physical and the spiritual (or mental/emotional). For instance, years ago, while at a conference for music teachers, I attended a session on Body Mapping, a therapeutic tool that brings together physical experience and artistic expression. Therapists use the technique in diverse settings, from working with victims of AIDS to helping musicians and dancers understand dysfunctions that inhibit their art. As described in the session I attended, therapists ask their patients to illustrate their body (or the affected part of their body, in the case of an injury or other physical dysfunction). Regardless of the degree of artistic talent, the process of putting pencil to paper allows the patient to better identify, describe, and understand physical pain and the emotional trauma that often accompanies that pain.

Other examples spring to mind. In college, I once crawled underneath the sink in my bathroom in order to stimulate creative thought and push through writer's block. (It worked, by the way.) My son relieves stress by playing his more energetic piano pieces very loudly and rapidly, with lots of arm pounding and foot tapping, his body swaying as his mind breaks free. My husband laces his spiritual lessons with insights gained on the football field.

I recently ran into what was, for me, a surprising connection between the physical and the emotional/spiritual. David Schnarch, a respected clinical psychologist and author, asserts that "sexuality is a powerful window into who we are," that our sexual attitudes and habits provide significant insight into our approach to life, and vice versa. I have thought, and even written, about that a fair amount...although most of that writing will never appear in this blog. His is an intriguing thought.

Whether in terms of sexuality or philosophical conundrums, artistry or athletics, I am beginning to glimpse a vision of the power behind the union of the body and the spirit. To re-phrase an oft-quoted scripture: "neither is the body without the spirit, nor the spirit without the body, in the Lord." Just as the harmonic blend of two voices produces a sound that transcends the reach of either voice on its own, we open ourselves to new vistas of emotional and physical possibilities when we work to unite body and spirit on equal terms.

One of THOSE Days

(October 2013)

I feel very fortunate to have dodged the clinical depression bullet. But every once in a while, melancholy descends briefly, leaving me in a tangled heap on the floor, tears hot on my cheeks. I fantasize about cutting a tiny X on my ankle, mostly just to feel the purity of the pain. I resist. Even on a dark day, I realize that some doors need to remain firmly closed. Eventually, I stand up and walk slowly from room to room, one foot in front of the other. I pick up a toy, start a load of laundry, wash a dish, tidy the pile of music in the front room. I am listless, but I begin to catch momentum. Then an email sets me off and I collapse again, wrapping my arms around my gut to embrace the stab of utter uselessness. Part of me stands apart, shaking my head at the silly dramatics that no one else sees in the empty house.

Years ago, on another day like this, I called home, needing my father's usual wisdom and comforting words. But Dad answered the phone in a bad mood, and I hung up quickly, feeling defensive and cheated. Prayer feels like that this week. God hears; I am sure of it. But He declines to answer, busy with more important things than my petty mood, or accurately recognizing that I can muddle through just fine on my own and need the experience anyway. I will agree with God tomorrow, probably even pulling some profound tidbit from the process. Today, though, I feel abandoned, my faith buried under cynicism.

Evening wallowing loses its charm after a while, so I exercise. For an hour or so, I can outrun or out bike the melancholy. As my legs pump and my heart beats, I feel strong. Endorphins push the gloom away, and I rise to the surface to take a deep breath. Before long, I will float to the top for good. By the time you read this, in fact, today's cynicism and gasping sobs will have faded into a memory of a day that I let the world win.

I hope I keep the memory, though, hope that in some way I can imagine these hours of melancholy stretching on for days or weeks. Then perhaps when I come across a friend buried under the waves, the heart that feels like stone now will find the empathy that I need to stretch out a hand. Perhaps I will stand on someone's porch, like a friend did for me today, not so much saying the words that needed to be said but offering a small patch of settled ground to help me gain my balance.

Sarah Laughed

(October 2013)

My husband reminded me that I left the story hanging with my last post ("One of THOSE Days"). "Aren't you going to write a follow-up post?" he asked. It was a momentous week, after all—surprising, humbling, a turning point. As I predicted, by the time I clicked Publish on my last post, I had found my equilibrium. The sun began to shine again, and peace returned. But it was only intermission. The story had yet to play itself out.

Do you remember the Old Testament account of Sarah and Abraham? Like most good Hebrew women, Sarah desired to raise children. To add strength to that perfectly righteous desire, God had promised Abraham that his posterity would be as the sands of the sea. And yet, not only did Sarah fail to conceive, but she had to watch her handmaid, Hagar, deliver Abraham's child in her place. For decades Sarah suffered the disappointment and shame of her childless condition, until at last she reached menopause. And then, one day she stood in the tent door listening while a holy man told Abraham, "Sarah thy wife shall have a son." What did Sarah do? She laughed to herself. The holy man promised the impossible; it was past time.

A couple of days before my recent fit of melancholy, I sat in the temple listening for the inspiration and answers that generally come to me there. The thought that tiptoed through my mind was a vision of Sarah and the gift of Isaac, a gift that came to her only after she had given up hope. Like Sarah, I had for decades desired a particular blessing. It was a perfectly righteous desire and, like Sarah, I had mostly given up hope of receiving that blessing. Mostly, but not quite. Recent events had rekindled just a spark of my hope, and the reminder of Sarah fanned the flame.

Sadly, the evening brought a resounding "no," seemingly straight from Heaven, and the loss of a newly revived hope sent me spiraling downward. My heart cracked just enough to let the faith drain out and the melancholy rush in to take its place. My husband flew to Utah on a trip that now seemed pointless, while I wallowed back at home. But sunshine and exercise, friends and the memory of faith lifted me. I still doubted my own ability to recognize inspiration, but I decided I could live without the desired blessing. After all, I had lived without it for years already.

In the midst of the calm, the phone rang. Astonishingly, the resounding "no" had turned to a "yes." Only after it was impossible did the blessing arrive. The next day, some of the people I love best of all stood together in one of the places I love best. Back home, I smiled. God remembered Sarah, even though she laughed, just as God remembered Rachel and millions of other covenant women. And God remembered me. It feels good to be remembered. I am humbled that I dared to think my Father would forget me.

It occurs to me that I have not, in fact, really told the rest of the story. After all, most of the telling belongs to other actors in the scene. Truth be told, I suspect that in the end this episode will prove to be just a small part of a tale that continues to unfold. But it is enough to remind me that my notions of possibility can hardly hem in the God of the Universe.

Advice to Myself

(December 2014)

For the past few months, I have served as the president of the women's organization in our congregation. I watch over roughly 200 women. Many of these women remain a mystery to me, names on the rolls but unresponsive to our efforts to reach out to them. Others are women I love, women I have counted as close friends for years and with whom I have served and laughed, worshipped and wept.

Somewhat of a recluse by nature, I appreciate that this calling forces me to seek out other women, moving beyond the comfortable routine of my life and away from my favorite spot on the back row. Often, I am privy to both the minutiae and the momentous in the lives of my sisters, feebly offering counsel when they request it, as if they think that by virtue of my office I have somehow stumbled upon a store of wisdom previously beyond my reach. I observe as they offer service to one another and as they discover their own talents and power in that service. Those moments inspire me.

There are other moments, too, when I walk into the darker valleys with these women. Because I work with the bishop of our congregation in order to lift the families and the women we serve, I learn much about their struggles. And herein lies today's dilemma. Perhaps the grey clouds this week have filtered my vision, but I begin to see primarily pain and illness, disappointment and sadness in the world around me. Jobs refuse to materialize, bank accounts fail to balance, illness stubbornly clings to those who are weary of its presence, children flail against the enormity of all that life expects of them, parents and friends stand by helpless. And I, it seems, have nothing to give them. I offer an ear or a prayer but little of any tangible value.

At the same time, my perspective shifts, and I have yet to determine if the shift is a positive one. Like those I serve, I chafe at a reality that often fails to match up to my expectations. I want to live within my means. I want to eat more responsibly. I want to reach toward my potential and achieve something wonderful, instead of slogging through each day just to accomplish a couple of the "must dos" on my checklist. But as I look around me, I begin to tell myself that to dream about that potential is foolhardy. I have a good life, a wonderful family, so many blessings that others will never have. To want more, to expect more, out of life would be ungrateful, perhaps even unkind, and certainly selfish.

At times like these grey days, I find I have to give myself the same advice I would give anyone else:

- Keep dreaming. Dream big and do not apologize for it. Be willing to sacrifice lesser things for your dreams. Family and faith are not lesser things.

- If something about your body bothers you, you probably already know what you need to do about it. Stop making excuses and do it! If there is something beyond your ability to fix, learn to love it.

- Illness happens. Depression happens. To everyone. Remember that God gets it, that He knows exactly how you feel and that He cares. He may not take the burden away, but He can make you strong enough to bear it, and He will truly help you to shoulder the load. Remember that others also struggle under burdens of physical and emotional illness. Reach out to them with the empathy your struggles have given you. That empathy is a gift to be used.

- Love those around you. Truly love them. Remember that God loves them way more than you do, and that He will watch over them just as He watches over you. You do not have the responsibility or usually the capability to solve their problems. That's OK. Just be there for them when you can and pray for them when you cannot.

- Ask for miracles. Expect them. Understand that they may not appear exactly according to your design or in your timetable, but know that the miracles will come in a way and a time that are best suited for you. Look for them and express gratitude for each and every miracle you see.

- If you are trying your best to do the right thing, to be in tune with the Spirit, to find the path God wants you to be on, then keep moving forward. It will all work out, even though right now you walk through a fog.

Control Freak on a Tightrope

(February 2015)

My husband stayed home from work today. I love my husband, truly I do. But today I needed the house to myself. I needed the inside of my brain uncluttered, without the rest of the world crowding in. I intended to exercise myself into a good, stinky sweat, then shower and settle down at the computer with a lovely pot of herb tea and write. I intended to ignore both phone and email, rebel against my incredibly annoying "to do" list and try to pull something profound out of my head. Ta da! In a week of appointments and work and children home on holiday, today was the one day that offered a clean slate and an empty house.

Sigh. Did I mention that I love my husband?

Did I also mention that I am currently suffering from a temporary case of writer's block, seasoned with a dash of ongoing limbo and served up on a dish of winter that stubbornly refuses to give way to spring in quite the timeframe I had hoped? And there you have the crux of the matter, if I am to give way to perfect honesty. I have run smack against a bit of life I cannot control, and I find myself thoroughly cross with the situation.

It is a bit of a tightrope, this tension between control and delicious surprise. On one side of the wire, I plot my life hour by hour on a calendar, depend on my grocery app and keep a detailed "to do" list, sorted by priority and date. As backup, I refer to two white boards in my kitchen: one for those things I really, really need to remember in case I forget to look at my task list and the other for chores the children need to accomplish before any fun ensues. I assume the overflowing junk drawers (not one, but two) in the kitchen help to offset the rigidity of the white boards.

On the other side of the wire bubbles an insistent need to escape the list app, pull out of routine and allow myself the luxury of the unknown, the unplanned. Sometimes I long to hang on to the boat and ride the waves, ready to gasp in delight at the breathtaking view around the bend. I find that the best moments usually lurk outside of my orchestration. But to surrender to another conductor requires a trust that I find difficult to muster with any frequency. So I long for order and crave random and find myself attempting to balance between the two.

When Nick Wallenda crossed the Grand Canyon on a tightrope 1500 feet above the canyon floor, he held a 30-foot-long, 43-pound flexible pole in his hands. The heavy pole held his center of gravity toward the safety of the steel cable and kept him from leaning dangerously far in either direction.

And me? I have that husband (whom I love), four wonderful children (whom I also love), and a dog (which I tolerate). They require meals at regular intervals and rides according to schedule. We have a comfortable routine of morning prayer and bedtime hugs. And when the routine leans threateningly toward monotony, I can count on the unexpected to pull me back to center. The dog will vomit on the carpet just before company arrives. Snowmen will require building after a spring storm. Impromptu chats with a teenage son will last for hours. Calls for service will shatter my schedule. And sometimes, on a quiet winter day when I had other plans, my husband will stay home from work.

Holding the Pose

(April 2015)

I do yoga on Saturdays. To say that I look forward to my Saturday ritual with great excitement might be overstating it a bit. More accurately, I procrastinate. I find clothes that need folding or messes that need straightening. News begs to be read and bathrooms beg to be scrubbed. I love the way I feel when I finish a yoga workout. I am less enthusiastic about the workout itself.

One cannot hurry yoga. Breathing must flow steady and slow, down to the bottom of the lungs. Breathe into the pose. Inhale. Exhale. Again. And again. All the while, my bad shoulder shakes underneath me in side plank. My thigh screams after several minutes of holding various warrior poses. My mind wanders to the next event on my schedule or the child who has climbed to the top of my worry list for the day. "You must reach equanimity," my instructor reminds me. "Calm your mind. Approach tension and allow it to release."

Brilliant idea. Find the tension. Breathe into it. Focus my vision. Allow my mind to calm, my face to relax. Sometimes I actually achieve a measure of equanimity. I flow from one pose into another, and it feels natural. I feel my spine realign itself as I open into side triangle pose, sternum and face reaching toward the ceiling. Ah!

And then, I reach a pose like upward bow pose, a pose that requires me to hold a back bend, surrendering my head and shoulders to gravity. For some reason, the bow pose makes me feel incredibly vulnerable. On days when equanimity proves elusive, the pose almost frightens me a little, although I doubt I could pinpoint the root cause of the fear. Failure, perhaps? Certainly not bodily harm, as extricating myself from the pose is an easy task. Something about relinquishing control of my head and neck makes my breath quicken and my heart rate increase. Pride comes to my aid, and I complete the pose once, twice, three times in the course of today's workout, refusing to give in. My muscles are up to the task. My back is flexible enough. Only my brain balks at the exercise. So I count my breaths, focus on a spot on the back wall and try not to think about the fear.

Life feels a little like bow pose sometimes. There is nothing inherently dangerous about my life. We enjoy good health. We pay our bills. Our cars run most of the time. The kids generally make good decisions and live exemplary lives. And yet, occasionally I have a day like today when I wake up feeling overwhelmed by the uncertainty of life. We continue to take steps in the dark, not yet sure of the right path for our family. People I love struggle with problems I cannot solve. I find myself needing to surrender control to the choices of others, to the will of God, to the vagaries of life.

"Live in the present," I tell myself. "Breathe in and out. Relax into life."

Because here's the secret. Yoga is not about becoming more flexible. It is not about finishing the workout and moving on. It is not about being stronger and twistier than the girl on the next mat. Yoga is all about the pose, about finding calm in tension and focus in distraction. And life is not really about knowing where I will live next year and what mission will give my life purpose and direction. Life, like yoga, is all about the pose. I take stock of where I am right now, stretching what needs to be stretched, finding center, and breathing through the movement from one phase into the next. When I feel the fear rise, I acknowledge the tension. I approach it, taking what steps I can, and then I focus my vision, count my breaths and surrender, all the while searching for equanimity.

Making Sense of the World

People Watching

(August 2010)

Daniel Schorr died recently. I always loved listening to his commentaries on NPR. Consequently, on my next trip to the library, I headed over to the biography section, intent on learning more about this man who has piqued my interest over the years. Obviously, someone else had the same idea. No biography available on our dear Mr. Schorr. Undeterred, I began to browse the biography racks for other gems. I knew I would find a handful in short order. At some point in the last decade I discovered that I love biographies, and that my enjoyment of the book has very little to do with any previous affinity for its subject. I imagine that realization came about the time I devoured a biography of the drummer for The Doors. I can name exactly one Doors song ("Light My Fire," naturally), and even now I have to turn to Google to give me the name of the drummer (John Densmore, in case you needed that information in order to be complete). Nonetheless, I found the book fascinating.

I suppose I simply love the back stories behind the faces of humanity. I love the joys of discovering nobility in unexpected places and the insights I gain from other folks' triumphs and tragedies, even the small day-to-day ones. With that in mind, I've been thinking of some biographies I would like to read, some people who have crossed my path and left behind a question mark.

Obvious names come to mind, of course. Someday, I want to read the real story of Joseph the Carpenter, not just the few verses in the Bible that mention him or the myths created about him in an effort to preserve Mary's virginity for all time. And I want to read the story of my grandmother, Florence, who died long before my birth. (Note: I *can* read that one, actually, because I published that biography in 2015!)

I also want to read about the 30-something man with a bright blue t-shirt who stood by the roadside yesterday holding a sign that read "will work for living expenses." He wore a baseball cap tilted just over his eyes and looked for all the world like a suburban dad on a Saturday morning.

Maybe someday I will stumble across a memoir by my college roommate. I lost track of her after that first year of college. I ran around with the

Honors group, and she danced on the dance line. Our circles rarely crossed. I heard some years ago that her husband died in the early years of their marriage. We have that in common, and I often wonder how that tragedy affected her.

Half a world away and years later, Steven Koch successfully became the first person to snowboard down the highest peaks on all seven continents. Anyone that crazy must have a fascinating biography out there. In fact, given the expenses he must have incurred in the process of peak hopping, I am quite certain I could purchase his story for a small fee. I should do that.

Also thousands of miles from my sleepy Midwestern town, a Jainist nun named Mataji caught the eye of a journalist for the Washington Post. Mataji and her fellow nuns live an ascetic life, renouncing all possessions and, indeed, all attachments to any thing or any person. These nuns walk, barefoot, for years, brushing the ground before their feet to avoid killing even a bug along their path. At the end of their lives, the women take sallekhana, essentially starving themselves to death in a ritual designed to bridge them into the next life. I am intrigued with the motivations and life experiences that bring a young woman like Mataji to such an extreme devotion.

And finally, I wish for a biography I will never have the chance to read. Eighteen years ago, my husband died of cancer at the age of 25. I would love to read about the man he never had the chance to become. As I watch our son grow, I begin to understand how little I knew his father. I would like to know him.

The Most Beautiful Woman in the World
(January 2011)

Years ago I heard someone say that at some point in her life, even if only for a moment in time, every woman is the most beautiful woman in the world. I think of that quote periodically as I gaze on humanity around me, and occasionally I have the wonderful opportunity to glimpse some of those "most beautiful woman in the world" moments.

Just last week, for instance, I sat chatting comfortably with a friend in her living room. As usually happens, our conversation meandered from God to pets to our own insecurities and on to those people who have influenced our life in significant ways. My friend does not consider herself beautiful. In fact, she isolates herself somewhat with the worry that her physical struggles will make others uncomfortable. Yet as she spoke of her mother, of their closeness and of the legacy of faith her mother left behind, tears wet her cheeks and a singular beauty stole over her countenance. I wish she could have seen herself at that moment.

Back in Vermont, I served in a presidency with my friend Jen, a woman who prefers to stride through life with her tough side turned out. I used to love watching the transformation she periodically exhibited (quite against her will, I think) in our meetings. With Jen, one can read the mood of the day by her clothing. Black does not signal joviality. On one particular day, I walked into the room to find my friend dressed in black, dark eye shadow to match the decided frown on her lips, arms folded and a personal bubble the size of Texas radiating out from her glare. We began the meeting with our usual prayer and proceeded to discuss the needs of the women under our care. I stole a glance at Jen now and then. Soon, she began to melt. The face relaxed, the bubble began to recede just a smidge, the arms dropped, and she leaned forward almost imperceptibly. Cursed with a high sense of duty and a heart far too big for her own comfort, Jen cannot long resist a peaceful spirit. The melting ice revealed a beautiful woman.

My friend Trisha also suffers the curse of a high sense of duty. With a large family and stewardship over hundreds of women, she gracefully carries the weight of responsibility, yet feels the stress of gifting out her time and energy in pieces to the hefty demands of each day. The other day, however, I noticed something different about her. She seemed lighter, at peace, more whole. A weekend with the girls, away from all the "shoulds" of her daily life, had generated a spa effect. Always lovely, just then she was the most beautiful woman in the world.

I think of other beautiful woman moments I have witnessed. My mother laughs freely with her granddaughter, their bond unmistakable. My young voice student finishes her first recital, the thrill of the moment in decided contrast to her original terror at the thought of performing in public. Filled with inspiration, Jen teaches a Sunday lesson to the young women she has served with love, her whole countenance shining with her conviction of their potential.

Gabriela Mistral, the Chilean poet, said once, "Love beauty; it is the shadow of God on the universe." I find that the search for those shadows infuses my life with divine moments.

Life in the News Feed
(May 2012)

I went for a bike ride the other day and, as often happens when I ride alone without music in my ear, I found myself composing my morning in the form of a Facebook status. I condensed my glorious ride amid the cornfields into various haikus extolling the wonders of birdsong and the relative merits of prairie wind and New England hills in building strong lungs and muscles. Pure poetry, I tell you. I almost never post my mid-exercise poetic ramblings for public consumption (or, rather, the consumption of those lucky 308 people subjected occasionally to my mutterings on their news feed). However, I find it amusing that I think of my life in those terms.

A friend of mine once found herself in the uncomfortable spotlight of an ongoing news event. As the spokesperson for one side of a political issue, she saw her views reduced to 10-second sound bytes. She would respond to interview questions thoughtfully, only to discover hours later that the sound byte that made the evening news gave a distressingly skewed vision of her stance.

I find the Facebook news feed somewhat akin to the 10-second sound byte: life condensed into a phrase or two. However, in social media I retain control over my 10 seconds of fame (unless, of course, my teenage son sneaks onto my account). Control is a wonderful thing, though with the control comes also the necessity of taking responsibility for that passionate outburst posted in the heat of frustration. Oops.

The sociolinguist in me loves the alternately fascinating and annoying window into a filtered world that social media provides. I have a host of people from various phases of my life that I now recognize in snippets, like the vision of a party illuminated in the pulse of a strobe light. Mark builds a marvelous collection of photos from his daily commute into Boston. A host of friends poke fun at life with a sardonic wit that leaves me laughing to myself in an empty house in the middle of the morning. A former student of mine sailed around the world this spring and posted pictures that inspire me with possibilities.

On the other hand…well, I will spare you my diatribe against emotional exhibitionism, poorly researched political scare tactics, the endless minutiae of health woes, and those awful "copy this into your status if you want to end world hunger/support abused children/tell your mother you love her" statuses that leave you feeling like a heartless guttersnipe for scoffing and refusing to re-post. Men and women have died for the right to freedom of speech. Who am I to trample on that freedom just because my news feed occasionally makes me cringe and wish for the days of stone tablets?

I suppose that in the short term, until social media gives way to another cultural phase, I will continue to frame my life in random chunks of thought. This week's snapshot, for instance? "Strawberry picking with my fellow crazy ladies. Laughter and freezer jam cure a multitude of ills."

The Best and Brightest

(July 2012)

"You are a chosen generation," we tell them. "God saved His best and brightest to send down to earth for these winding up scenes." In twenty years of teaching teenagers, I have delivered such lessons dozens of times. We sense, at times, the urgency of our days, the need for strong leaders and noble hearts. We know how much the world requires of our youth, and we attempt to inspire them, to motivate them upward to the great heights we hope they can reach.

And then, almost in the next breath, we take those visions of greatness and sweep them out of reach. We begin to make excuses for the youth, for ourselves. They are so tired. They face such great temptations. Consider the homes in which they live: the physically or emotionally absent fathers, the abuse, the difficult finances. They work so hard to meet the demands of schoolwork, that to expect more out of them would be unfair. You know the routine because you have made those same excuses for your own children and for others.

I do not have the answers. But I know that if we want these youth to reach the heights, we need to set them on the path, and we need to give them the tools to climb. We cannot climb for them and then feed them cookies while we show them photos from the top of the mountain. Nor can we sip our cocoa and shove them out the door to go climb the mountain on their own, only to grumble at their failure when they turn back before they reach the summit.

Yousef Karsh, the famous photographer, started life in Turkish Armenia. When just 14 years old, he fled the Armenian genocide and eventually landed in Canada. He lived with an uncle, who recognized and nurtured his talent. From humble beginnings, Yousef built a successful career photographing influential leaders and celebrities all over the world. His iconic portrait of Winston Churchill glared from the cover of Life Magazine in May 1945, earning him rare praise from the prime minister, who said, "You can make even a roaring lion stand still to be photographed."

One biographer described the 20-something Yousef as "young, talented and hungry." That phrase caught my eye. Hunger, both physical and metaphorical, represented a key ingredient in Yousef's success. I thought of other hungry youth who used their challenges as a motivation to success: Stephen Hawking, Oprah Winfrey and Franklin Delano Roosevelt, to name just a few.

Victor and Mildred Goertzel researched hundreds of the world's most influential people for their classic book *Cradles of Eminence*. Three quarters of their research subjects sprang from troubled childhoods. Over one quarter succeeded despite serious physical handicaps. The Goertzels concluded, among other things, that the drive to compensate for disadvantages actually propelled these individuals to their eventual success. In essence, hunger led to greatness.

How, then, do we recognize and nurture that hunger into a positive force? Even more difficult, how do we awaken motivating hunger in youth stifled by complacency? If our youth are to rise to great heights, they first have to dream. They need a reason to look upward. Clearly, the answer does not lie in manufacturing tragic circumstances for our children. Neither does it lie in shielding them from every difficulty or immediately fixing every problem for them.

We can give them space to design and build, fail and fly. We can cheer their successes and hug them through their failures. We can chase our own dreams and share them. Above all, we can expect much and love much.

Beginning, Middle and End

(September 2013)

We recently renegotiated our satellite dish contract, a lovely little dance we engage in once a year when they raise our monthly fee. Consequently, we received a few weeks of free movie channels, the company's way of saying "thank you" for buying into dozens of channels we need about as much as we need a hundred bottles of Marshmallow Fluff. I rarely watch television, but it does provide a good motivator on those days when I exercise indoors. While my husband plays heavy metal during a workout, I find the distraction of a good movie helps me bring my knees a little higher and push the weight a little longer. Nothing says "Work it, girl!" like *Dr. Who* or *Sense and Sensibility*.

I have enjoyed this temporary break from Netflix and the chance to watch a few movies I would have forgotten to watch otherwise. I do have one complaint, however. Unless I time my exercise just right (simply not gonna happen), I end up watching portions of movies and rarely catch the story from beginning to end. I start a movie with just half an hour left of my workout and realize with a sigh that I will never find out whether Sandra Bullock finally gives in to Hugh Grant's charm or whether aliens win the war they have waged against a future earth. (Oh wait, aliens never win those, do they? And everyone eventually gives in to Hugh Grant; he's just that charming.)

Having watched the beginnings of some movies and the endings of others, I have decided that, if I have to choose, I am definitely a "start in the middle and see the end" kind of girl. There is something so very satisfying about a conclusion, particularly one that someone else designed. If I come in at the middle of the story, I can imagine the beginning, putting together the pieces from the dialogue and the story as it continues. But imagining an end to the story in my head feels like cheating. Besides, while I can turn a phrase now and again, conclusions have always given me fits. I tend to end my pieces rather abruptly, without much elegance or substance. Give me another writer's twists and turns and winding up scenes, and I will watch happily while applauding their brilliance. I might even shed a tear or two if I am feeling particularly hormonal.

I suppose I apply this penchant for conclusions to my outlook on life, as well. At the risk of sounding apocalyptic, I love the thought of living in the winding up scenes of the world, a time when the history and philosophy, the literature and science, the art and music and religion of thousands of years blend together in glorious ways. I even have a few story lines in mind that I hope to see through to the end.

- For instance, I know the path involves devastating wars and impossible heartache, but I want to see Isaac and Ishmael come together again to honor their father Abraham, as they did once long ago in the field of Ephron (Genesis 25:9). Come to think of it, there are a few more brothers and sisters who could stand to come together in Ephron and remember a common heritage. God, for reasons of His own, may seem to favor one person or group over another in the short term, but that hardly gives us an excuse to do the same.

- On the national political scene, I hope to live to see some wise recess monitor teach the boys and girls in the Congressional playground to play well together. After two hundred years of setting the rules, they seem to have forgotten the basics.

- Our world has evolved quite far from that first garden. I look forward to a day when we as a people evolve enough to remember the commission to take care of the garden, to cherish both our Eden and the plants and animals that grow there.

- Technology that seemed fantastical science fiction decades ago has become a reality. Perhaps I will never have the chance to give the "beam me up, Scotty" ready call, but I hope to see the day when I can travel the world—and even the stars—by miraculous means.

And, though I probably will not live to see the end of the world as we know it, there is part of me that dreams of waking up on that day when everything has changed. Back in my singing days, I used to sing a wonderful spiritual called "My Lord What a Morning," and in my mind I can just catch a glimpse of that day "when the stars begin to fall." I can feel a bit of the wonder, breathe a bit of that new air. I imagine the stars will fall long after I have moved on, and I will find I have lived the middle of the movie, after all. But, when it comes to the heart of the matter, most endings are simply the beginning of a new story.

Those Things You Should Never Say

(February 2014)

I find myself deeply indebted to social media for an education that would paralyze me into silence…if I were more empathetic and politically correct. This morning, I read yet another "10 Things You Should Never Say to…" article, and something snapped. I took a little Google tour, searching on "things never to say" (an enlightening journey). I stopped at 20 pages of articles but could have trolled the internet for hours to learn what not to say to your fishing partner, your co-workers, vegetarians, a grieving spouse, a gay person, an American, a Chicano, a dog owner, flight attendants, a redhead, someone you are breaking up with, a transgender person, people with curly hair (really?)…and my personal catch-all favorite: "Ten Things Never to Say to Other People. Period." The overwhelming majority of the articles relate to moms of all shapes and sizes and stages: expectant moms, working moms, stay at home moms, single moms, parents of special needs children, parents of triplets, moms of boys, Filipino parents, new moms over 40, new moms under 25, stressed-out parents.

Having been a pregnant woman, a grieving spouse, a working mom, a stay at home mom, and a hundred other "someones," I thought I should probably take a look at some of the utterances that any thinking person should have known never to say to me at that particular period of my life.

Apparently, I should have taken great offense as a working mother if anyone told me that I looked exhausted. Ooh, well. The fact of the matter is that I *was* exhausted. My one-year old seemed to catch every childhood illness that breathed its way through daycare. I travelled frequently. Management duties kept me up at night when the baby did not. Yep, I had days when my eyes wanted nothing more than to close for just a few seconds of quiet bliss. You would have been an idiot not to notice, and it is OK that you mentioned it. I found myself even more exhausted as a stay at home mom, and it is OK that you noticed then, as well. The working mother blogger supported her plea for inoffensive comments with her assertion that "I am no different than anyone else." All right, sweetie, I'll take you at your word and stop tip-toeing around you.

Hundreds of sites list terrible things never to say to a pregnant woman. Well yes, let's walk right into that mine field. Give a woman an overload of hormones and a few inches around the tummy and thighs (and arms and cheeks and ankles) and there really is no way to be sure you will say the right thing. Most of us cry and huff and puff and eventually get over the questions and advice once the hormones have subsided. One blog author differentiated between the childless person who offends with the comment "get all the sleep you can now" and the new parent who appropriately commiserates with the very same comment. Hmm…what if that childless person deals with infertility and is simply trying her best to relate to you in a condition she will never have, no matter how much she wants a child? I am quite certain that one of those 10 Things You Should Never Say to a Person Who Can't Conceive runs along the lines of "You wouldn't understand because you have never had a child."

As a 20-something widow, I appreciated the fact that a select group of people actually *could* empathize with my situation and knew instinctively what to say. At the same time, I appreciated all of the bumbling attempts to connect with me by friends and strangers who knew they could never say the right thing but wanted to open their mouth in support anyway. Thank you for not letting your fear of casting offense keep you from walking across the room to speak to me. I know how long that walk can be, how you rehearse in your mind what you will say to the wounded woman who feels a pain you may never experience.

One snarky blogger ended her post with a statement that brought her a little redemption in my eyes. "The questions and words should not be filled with judgment but with support." Yes, yes! Exactly. If you want to be helpful, tell me what I should say in support instead of automatically assuming I mean to be judgmental. I do not (well, most of the time, anyway). Generally, I genuinely want to connect with those around me who deal with addictions, depression, stress, illness and a host of other challenges that life throws at all of us. I try my best. I fail a lot. And I will continue to believe that freezing in silent fear of saying the wrong thing is generally much worse than reaching out my hand in love and trying my best to connect with another human being.

Friendship

Forgiveness

(August 2010)

This past spring I offered forgiveness to a woman who had been, at one time, a close friend. She neither requested nor acknowledged my forgiveness, but it didn't matter. My gesture was, in a sense, selfish, born out of a desire to rid myself of the burden of bad feeling. I hardly understood my feelings about my erstwhile friend as they simmered under the surface for months, clouded as they were by a mist of deceit and hinted complexities.

Were it not for my 4-year old daughter and her increasing references to this woman who had once worked her way so deeply into our lives, I could have buried my frustration. But 4-year olds, particularly when prompted by forces beyond adult comprehension, exhibit a remarkable tenacity. With every reference to Jane's house, Jane's pigs, the day we went swimming with Jane, the sliver worked deeper underneath my fingernail.

I craved emotional freedom, and as I pondered, I realized my only path to that freedom was to forgive. I pleaded with God for the power to do just that. Although I knew I needed to forgive Jane, I could scarcely articulate, even to myself, what I needed to forgive her for. Slowly and surely, however, the forgiveness flowed through me. I remember the day I sat down and wrote a message to Jane, asking forgiveness for those things I knew angered her and offering my forgiveness in return. I clicked Send and settled back in my chair, knowing I would receive no answer but already feeling the lightness. Oddly, my daughter has not mentioned Jane to me since then.

In the past weeks, I learned more about Jane and the actions she took after our friendship. Finally, I saw with clarity exactly what I needed to forgive, offenses I had not suspected before. The clarity should have overwhelmed me, should have chipped my armor. Instead, I felt a remarkable calm, an unexpected and beautiful peace. God, in His infinite grace, granted me the power to forgive in advance of my knowledge, so that when I most needed peace, His peace enveloped me.

Of Friendship and the Cadence of Life

(October 2010)

Some years ago, a new friend of mine surprised me one day by announcing that she had determined I was "above the fold." Laughing a bit at herself, she explained a philosophy that sounds arrogant at first but holds significant wisdom. The gist of the "above the fold" philosophy of friendship, as I have come to understand it, is this. Most of us meet a great many people in the span of our lives. Sheer logistics dictate that we cannot count them all among our bosom buddies, nor can we spend equal time and emotional energy on each and every relationship. Just as newspaper editors place key stories above the physical fold of the paper, we sometimes need to determine which friendships are key relationships in our lives.

For me, these are the friends I deliberately choose to spend time with, those whose advice I seek and value, the companions I would invite to my vacation home...if I had one. I dare say some of these people would be surprised to find themselves above the fold on my list of friends. I avoid talking on the phone, value my time alone, and have proven terrible at maintaining long distance relationships. Still, when I pick up the phone to find an unexpected voice from long ago on the other end, the years melt away, and I relax into the familiar cadence of an interrupted conversation.

A recent birthday call took me back to Memorial Day weekend, 1992. April had flown into town from Houston for a visit. In our fifteen years of friendship, I had often played the wise big sister role. This time, however, April sensed my need for perspective and dragged me up the canyon for a quick camping trip. We left my toddler son and terminally ill husband in the care of my in-laws.

Finding all the official campgrounds full for the holiday weekend, we set up camp in a quiet spot near the "gnome caves." Long after dark, we built a roaring campfire and talked of life and death in the philosophical way of twenty-somethings coming face to face with mortality. We laughed over the pages of Robert Fulghum's "All I Really Need to Know I Learned in Kindergarten," and I returned home the next day buoyed up enough to carry on for another week or so.

More recently, I sat with friends over lunch, chatting casually about the momentous and the inconsequential in our lives. I have known these three women for barely a year, and we spend little time together. Occasionally, we day trip to St. Louis or catch up with one another at book group. Still, the conversation was easy, comfortable. I trust these women, know instinctively that I could safely cry with them, serve with them, or celebrate with them. Their association gives me strength.

Even Jesus, though he was the Savior of all mankind and associated with lepers and noblemen alike, found refuge in a few close friendships. Though the crowds followed him, and though he took the time to bless and heal, to seek out the lost sheep, when the Savior of the world craved solace himself, he went fishing with Peter or dined with Lazarus and his sisters.

Over a period of decades, I have gradually internalized this concept of the need for friendships that nourish the soul. Not until my 30s did I begin to truly understand the value of close girl friends—not just women to hang out with, but confidantes. Through a number of years of early morning walks and monthly foodfests over a Scrabble board, I came to depend upon those confidantes. I also learned, through trial and sometimes painful error, to trust my own rhythms when it comes to relationships. Those rhythms bring music to my life.

Building Blocks
(November 2010)

I have been thinking today about some of the people who have significantly influenced my life over the years, trying to sort out the various facets of my personality and attitudes and determine their source.

My parents have obviously wielded immense influence, primarily through their examples. Three main lessons come to mind, however. Seek knowledge. Be interested in, not just tolerant of, people from all backgrounds. Maintain integrity always. Yeah, always. Even when it embarrasses your teenage children who would prefer a graceful white lie.

I have one sister, five years older than I. We stand the same height, and my children think we sound alike (particularly in our sarcastic moments).

Beyond that, the similarities fade. Sylvia left home when I was 13 and thoroughly self-absorbed. I have recognized her influence more as an adult. Her overall calm and her example as a mother to an amazing family have inspired me. I have never managed to match the calm, but I have aspirations...

College was a pivotal time for me, as it should be, and Chris was a huge part of my university life. He is one of those larger than life characters who draw a following, and it took a few years for me to realize, somewhat to my embarrassment, that he played a much greater role in my life than I did in his. Be that as it may, our friendship in a sense embodied those college years for me. I learned to challenge boundaries, not just societal boundaries, but also those within myself. I also learned that life and love are messy, and that is just fine. Creativity is a messy process.

Not all of my life lessons came from comfortable sources. While my friendship with Jane (not her real name) died some time ago, I remain indebted to her for invaluable lessons about what friendship is...and what it is not, or at least what it cannot be for me. I learned to respect my limits, and I learned not to dive headfirst into someone else's life and problems. Years ago, I sat on my bed one evening and wailed, "But I wanted it to be a happy day!" I have never relinquished that childhood wish. I still long for a happy day, not only for me but for those around me. I cannot fix everyone's problems. The bare fact of the matter remains that often the healthiest solution for all involved is to simply stand back and let people climb their own mountains. Sometimes we walk alongside and cheer them on. Sometimes we toss them a canteen. And sometimes we turn our backs and claw the way up our own trail.

I grew up with Mother, and I gained Mom with my first marriage. Although she calls herself the "outlaw" now, I will always consider Kathryn family. I often echo her counsel that "things done when thought of need no further attention." My children listen about as well as her son did, but at least I remind myself of the counsel on a regular basis. Also from Kathryn, I have learned that tears can be a gift. I have watched and felt the marvelous effect of her tears in softening hearts that need to feel and releasing tears from dry eyes that need to weep.

We named Kristina after two of her grandmothers, both because we loved the names and in order to remind her of her rich heritage. I watch from across the room as she plays hide-and-go-seek over the phone with her Grandma Ruth. How they play over the distance of 1000 miles, I will never understand, but they share a special bond. I admire Ruth's unconditional love for her family and her dedication to each of us.

I was raised by liberal parents who set an example of sticking firmly to standards while accepting and celebrating the diversity around them. While I once prided myself on internalizing that principle, I have come to realize that my husband far outstrips me in his genuine interest in other people and his willingness and ability to accept them regardless of their degree of social acceptability. Brad frequently reminds me of the fact that God looks on the heart, that if we have the opportunity to catch a glimpse of heaven one day, we may find ourselves rather surprised at its inhabitants.

I met my friend Susan years ago when we both worked in Cache Valley, part of the bosom of the Mormon church. While not particularly religious herself, Susan exhibits charity and integrity more than almost anyone I know, reminding me that those attributes are not restricted to folks who are overtly religious. We all could use that reminder now and again, particularly when we make bold assumptions about a political candidate or a neighbor based on where they spend their Sunday mornings or what dogma they profess to follow.

Melissa and Heather brought exercise into my life, starting with daily walks while we passed Cheerios to our boys in their baby joggers and sustained each other through the ups and downs of life and motherhood. From those early morning walks, they pushed me to yoga and weightlifting, plyometrics, and beyond. I owe these women not only for their remarkable friendship but for a habit of exercise that has become essential to my well-being.

To the village who continues to raise this adult, I send a humble "thank you."

Pausing in Bethany

(April 2013)

Every spring, much of the Christian world celebrates Passion Week, commemorating the events of each day in the last week of the Savior's life. Regarding one day in that week, we know almost nothing. Two days before his death, Jesus returned to the village of Bethany, and for a whole day the scriptures fall silent. We can assume with some confidence that He spent that day quietly with his close friends Mary, Martha and Lazarus. With them, as with almost no one else, Jesus could relax, could find solace, could step aside from the world that clamored either for His healing touch or for His blood.

In the midst of events of eternal significance, Jesus more than once paused in Bethany. He ate dinner with friends. We know He wept with them. I like to think He laughed with them, as well, and perhaps told stories of His travels or listened to their thoughts and dreams. They served each other, walked together, almost certainly enjoyed moments of peaceful, companionable silence.

Recently, I spent a weekend getaway with three friends. While we hardly save the world, we do each lead lives of eternal significance. We build marriages, raise children or siblings, heal bodies and spirits, teach youth, create. Sometimes we feel the weight of our worlds resting heavily on our shoulders, and sometimes we feel tiny and insignificant.

The weekend passed comfortably, easily, like slipping into a favorite pair of pajamas and sipping a cup of hot chocolate on a lazy afternoon. Our hostess possesses an uncanny ability to create a sense of peace with carefully arranged furniture and art, and that peace pervaded the hours. We made meals together, chatting over the kitchen counter while we ate. We lounged on the sofa and laughed about our lives. We played at the park like my daughter and her friends (though without the cartwheels), browsed through local art stores, took silly photos, basked in moments of silence, and even played with makeup. We did nothing worthy of note to anyone but ourselves, and we ignored schedules.

I returned home rejuvenated, grateful for my life and grateful, as well, for the friendships that ground me and add color and depth to that life. Because sometimes, pausing in Bethany carries its own eternal significance.

Family

Of Blasphemy and Breathing

(September 2010 blog post, originally written in 2009)

I'm pretty much a straight arrow when it comes to the Commandments. Never been one to flirt with hellfire and damnation. Don't care to dodge lightning bolts, either. And yet, as the silence lengthened, and it became clear that he had breathed his last, ragged breath, I held Brady's hand and sighed, "God, I loved him." I wish I could say I was praying, but that would add another to the list of Top Ten Commandments broken for the afternoon. I swear more than I care to admit. But that "Thou shalt not take the name of the Lord thy God in vain" commandment? I'm scrupulous about that one. I remember three slip-ups in my entire life—remember them vividly, in fact, because I felt guilty about each and every one. This time, however, my blasphemy took me by surprise, profaning an otherwise incredibly spiritual synapse between life and death.

6:02 p.m. August 7, 1992. We gathered in the bedroom of my apartment. Brady's parents, his best friends, and I surrounded the hospital bed that Hospice had delivered a few days earlier. The head of the bed lay against the window as lazy-summer sunlight washed over the scene. After a couple of days of wrestling my incoherent and writhing husband, I had been almost relieved when the onset of coma brought rest to both of our weary bodies. The labored breathing and the ritual of the family keeping a death watch, however, sustained the tension all day.

Now, with Brady's breath stilled, the group of us around the bed gradually eased our own breathing, relaxing tentatively into the emerging peace. An expectant silence filled the apartment complex. Word must have spread that Brady's death was imminent, because our neighbors seemed to respectfully keep their distance. The mortician was a family friend. A day or two later we joked morbidly with him while we planned the funeral, but on that evening he remained subdued as he and his assistant took the body carefully down the stairs.

Our son, Devin, came home from the babysitter's after the mortician left, and my mother-in-law and I spent the evening alternating between toddler routine and shedding the trappings of illness and death. We sent the hospital bed away, poured bottles of medicine down the sink, washed bedding, removed the wheelchair, made phone calls, and hugged each other.

Years later and 2000 miles away, my young neighbor, Doug, wasted away with cancer. I remember glancing out my window one afternoon and noticing his wife riding her bike past our house—no helmet, wind blowing her hair back from her face. I knew immediately that Doug had died because I recognized that familiar, intangible sense of release surrounding his wife.

I had my own moments of release in those months after Brady's death, times when I'm sure my need for freedom jarred the sensibilities of family and friends who needed me to fit their own comfortable definition of "widow." My parents worried as I headed cross-country, pulling all my possessions in a rented trailer behind my red pickup truck. Colleagues at work back-pedaled, embarrassed, when their questions about my marital status finally elicited an explanation they had not expected. As a 25-year old professional, smiling and independent, I was not exactly a poster child for grieving widowhood.

As a matter of fact, I failed to fit my own definition of widowhood. Brady should not have died just three years into marriage, after I discovered his faults but before I gained the maturity to discard the illusion I married and admire his true strengths. He should not have died muddled by brain cancer, forgetting how to tie his tie, impatient with the toddler who had become his playground rival rather than his son. He should not have died before I learned how to forgive him for youthful bad decisions that had left me feeling betrayed.

One night, in the midst of those long months of illness, I knelt with my son to help him say his prayers. At my prompting, he asked God to make his daddy better. I watched his blond curls as he prayed, wishing I did not have to cheat like this, wishing I could say the prayer myself with the same fervor and faith. Surely I owed it to my husband to feel desperate for a miracle. Even in the disillusionment of early marriage, I know I never wished for his death. But, being the realist that I am sometimes, I did recognize stage-four glioblastoma as his death sentence. As a mother of a young child, I had to prepare for the future. So I let Devin pray for the miracle, knowing he was too young to comprehend the burden I placed on him. I also knew that he was too young to lose his faith when no ram bleated in the thicket at the last moment to save his father as the Old Testament ram saved Isaac.

Brady had a birthday last week, his 42nd. Devin, now off at college in Brady's hometown, called for directions to his father's gravesite. I can picture Devin standing in that quiet corner of the cemetery, poised in an awkward phase between youth and maturity. On that August evening, years ago, Brady was not so many years older than Devin, a far cry from the middle-aged man he would have been today.

With the perspective of decades, I think perhaps a sigh, once seemingly blasphemous, has become a grateful prayer. "God, I really did love him." And once again I breathe, no longer tentative about the peace.

Remembering
(August 2012)

20 years ago this week, I lost my husband. Silly phrase, that. I did not "lose" Brady, of course. I knew exactly where he was. He lay on the bed in front of me. After hours in a coma, heart racing and breathing ragged, he opened his eyes briefly, as if to note that the important people had gathered for his transition moment. We had--most of us, anyway. His cousin and close friend did not hear the news in time, and his sister lived far away, but Brady could wait no longer. He closed his eyes, drew one last breath and crossed a bridge, out of our sight for a time.

My father gave me a priesthood blessing that night. He blessed me, among other things, with the ability to do what I needed to do to wrap things up and leave my relationship with Brady behind until the eternities. At the same time, he reminded me that a closeness would continue and that Brady would always remain near, would always care.

I had forgotten the specifics of that blessing until I read my journal just now. Looking back with the perspective of time and experience, I see inspiration in my father's words. Brady and I shared just three years together as husband and wife. We were young and stupid, trying to be grownups and, more often than not, falling short.

Just two months after Brady died, I moved cross country, seeking fresh air and a chance to remember how to be young. I married again, a year and a half later. I have always wondered what Brady thought about that. Even though I knew without a doubt that I did the right thing, for a long time I still felt a twinge of guilt, a sense that I had betrayed Brady somehow, or at least that I had betrayed the sensibilities of his family.

I have visited his grave over the years, reporting in. "Devin is growing tall, Brady. He's smart and handsome. You would be so proud." And later, pleading, "Please help me raise your son. I'm trying my best, but he's struggling, and I feel so inadequate." Then, just a year ago, I sat in the Salt Lake temple with Devin for the first time. I prayed fervently that Brady could share in that moment somehow, that he could watch his son prepare to serve a mission, that he could see the fine man Devin had become.

Devin and others have sensed Brady's presence over the years. I never felt I deserved that experience. But I find myself, all these years later, wondering what it will be like to see him again. I hope we can be friends. I hope we can sit down and compare stories over a cup of hot chocolate. I hope we can take our grandchildren (or great-grandchildren) for walks in the clouds and argue about whether they inherited their intellect and talent from Grandma or from Grandpa.

In those early years, I wanted to wield my pen to write a stunning tribute to Brady. I soon realized how very little I knew him, that I would do better to raise his son well than to try and create a life that Brady himself had not yet lived. Now I find that I have nothing profound to say. In some way and in his own time, Brady will find a way to tell his own story. I do not pretend to understand eternity, and I cannot paint heaven. But I do know that Brady lives on. I know I will see him again, and I think he will smile when he sees me. I hope he does.

Until then, I will simply live my life. Now and then I will look up and wink at the sky. I will hear a snatch of a song or catch a glimpse of a Rocky Mountain sunset, and I will remember a life I had the honor to share just briefly.

Blatant Nostalgia Trip

(January 2011)

I am listening to Bonnie Raitt and lapsing into nostalgia this afternoon. I remember clearly the first time I heard one of her songs. It was early evening on August 12, 1992. Chris and I were driving up to Bear Lake for a raspberry shake, talking a little but mostly breathing and listening. I began to relax for the first time in weeks, maybe months. Still, I felt like an awkward teenager after a makeover, not sure quite what to make of the new self emerging, aware that others reacted differently to me now and unsure how to react to myself.

My parents and I argued on my return, Dad worrying about me joyriding with a married guy friend just hours after my husband's funeral. I don't imagine they realize, even now, how essential that evening was for me (and how innocent). Chris and I had always connected deeply and uniquely. I needed that instinctive connection just then--no explanations or discussion, just the permission to simply exist. I suppose I probably even needed the hint of rebellion and the release that came with the argument at home.

A few weeks later I packed my pickup truck and moved cross country to Vermont. As a parting gift, Sue gave me Bonnie's "Nick of Time" album for the drive. That album became a link to my past and the anthem of my rebirth. Even now, it transports me back to Saturday afternoons on Burlington's Church Street, my toddler son turning heads with his blond curls and hip sunglasses. Inspired by his delight, perhaps, I felt myself growing younger with the passing seasons. Months of caring for a terminally ill husband had aged me by decades. Now I felt the years falling away. I explored my new territory, fascinated both with the charm of Vermont and with the adjustments in my emotional landscape.

I loved those early years in Vermont--the fog over Lake Champlain on my way to work, the silliness of somersaulting into snowdrifts, my son singing behind me on the bike, the thrill of falling in love quite unexpectedly. Bonnie Raitt and rich New England air worked their magic on me, healing and rejuvenating, filling me to the brim with life. Even now, listening and remembering, I breathe a little more deeply and feel new.

Lost and Finding

(September 2010)

I began to lose sight of myself on an early summer evening five years ago when God dropped a boulder in my path. I had one foot on the threshold of the next phase of my life, just waiting for autumn when my youngest son would step on the school bus for the first time. I had plans, vague to be sure, but plans nonetheless. God had plans, too. They involved one last child and turning my clock back six years. I could have refused, but I know better than to invite the consequences of resisting divine will. So I reluctantly, angrily even, opened a door I had locked tightly behind me some years earlier.

Born eight weeks early, our daughter captured all of our hearts immediately. I fell in love with her, as I did with all of my children. But still I struggled with God's timing, fought against the direction my life had taken, and longed for the self I had intended to become. Before I regained my footing, troubled adolescence and ghosts from the past ripped the fabric of our family life. I found myself caught in a crossfire of struggling souls. Hurting for my son, my husband, and myself, one dark night I lashed out in desperation, dragging my fingernails across my face.

Before the wounds healed, when my bangs half-hid a red cross, my daughter stroked my forehead, trying to soothe the hurt. She never questioned, just comforted, and the heavens I once thought cold began gently to instruct. In my mind's eye, I replayed an oft-repeated scene.

In the midst of the crossfire, oblivious to the bullets, a little girl cries out in the pre-dawn hours. That early in the morning, her crib no longer satisfies her, but neither is she ready to tumble open-eyed into her day. Still weary myself, both from the early hour and the household tension, I lift her out of her crib and snuggle with her in the nursery bed. At first she lays her head on my shoulder and nuzzles deeply into my neck, melting into me. I wrap my arms around her in a tight hug, feeling her heartbeat slow as she settles back into sleep. I let the fuzzy top of her head caress my chin and cheek as I relax into the pillows, breathing in the faint scent of lavender left over from the previous night's bath.

After a time, my daughter begins to reach for wiggle room. I shift her out of my arms and place her cheek on the pillow next to mine. We lie there, foreheads touching and arms intertwined. I shift my head slightly to breathe in the air she exhales. Her breath smells sweet, innocent. I drift with my daughter into simple morning dreams, drops of healing elixir.

The elixir of innocent childhood healed all of us at times. The tension eased and changed form, but continued, exacerbated by Brad's new, out-of-state job and a house that refused to sell. I read somewhere that God tests us by asking us to surrender the very things we are most loath to hand over. I suspect my performance on that test failed to impress any casually watching angels. God asked for my time, my patience, and my willingness to stumble along in the dark, unable to direct my own course. I fumed, pleaded, despaired, gloried in epiphanies, occasionally wept in gratitude for tiny miracles, fumed again, and found hope in chance conversations and the wisdom of a patient husband.

Finally, the house sold, and we headed West to new adventures and space for deep, cleansing breaths. Caught up in the relief of calm vistas and peaceful nights, it took a few months for me to realize I had lost myself along the way. I began to feel the absence of identity and a need for goals to anchor me and provide me purpose. This time, I look upward and outward for cues, waiting a little more patiently and trusting a little more completely. Gradually, a new self begins to emerge, still slightly blurry around the edges but gathering clarity and strength.

Soap Operas and Bonbons

(August 2011)

With my first conscious thought this morning I pondered a long-forgotten question: What shall I do today? I have had little occasion to ask myself that question in the 23 years since I entered corporate life and then began building my family. I rolled the thought around my mind, tasting the deliciousness of the possibilities. Never mind that the actual play by play of my day reads like a rather mundane "to do" list. The very fact that *I* decide what makes the list and when I start and stop each task caused me to jump out of bed with a smile.

My youngest started kindergarten this week, darting off to the bus with a nervous grin and eyes sparkling with excitement. She gently but firmly informed us that she did not want us to accompany her to her class on the first day of school. So we took pictures before waving her off, and I returned to the quiet of an empty house.

I love my children, truly I do. And I love my husband. I also love my time alone.

I feel a bit of a kinship with my father this week. I believe he began planning for his retirement from the time he walked off the stage with his doctoral degree in hand. He enjoyed his careers, as far as I could tell, the teaching and speaking, anyway, if not the administrivia. But he had plans for that time when he determined the answer to his own "what shall I do today" question. Now here he is, living in a wonderful log house in a village in the mountains, teaching himself Greek and Hebrew, hiking and biking, volunteering, and (I hope) writing.

I have no aspirations to teach myself Greek and Hebrew. I do, however, have a book patiently waiting for me to write it and a blog suffering atrophy from my shameful neglect. I have Old Testament lessons to prepare for early morning seminary and muscles begging for regular exercise. I may even treat myself to a little non-required reading now and again. We all have our guilty pleasures, after all.

In the short term, when yet another person cheerfully asks what I plan to do with my newfound freedom, I will simply smile and say, "Soap operas and bonbons, of course."

Of Knights in Shining Armor

(January 2011)

My husband and I have an anniversary tomorrow, our 17th. I have been thinking lately about those things that have kept me happily married over the years. All too often, I take my husband for granted. And then sometimes a chance conversation with a friend reminds me how unusually blessed I am in this stubborn New Englander that I married.

17 years ago, Brad was a 21-year old sometime college student, living at home and working nightshift at IBM. I was older, a widow, a single mom, and a professional. Logic would never envision us together, but then, logic hardly has a corner on wonderful, does it? We went target shooting on our first date, paused to watch the sunset over Lake Champlain, then struggled to find a late-night dinner that would fit into my vegetarian lifestyle. I never intended to date him again, but I had not taken into account the Wallace charm. From guns to reggae to Hill Cumorah to Mozart, somehow I fell in love without intending to.

I celebrate my anniversary tomorrow because not only do I love my husband, but I rather like him, as well. After all these years, we still find ourselves talking for hours without struggling for words. I seek his advice, and often I even follow that advice. When laughter sends tears down my cheeks, or the sunrise dazzles the frost-covered trees along the road, I hurry to share the moment with Brad. Years ago, on vacation in Maine and sleeping peacefully, I felt a tap on my shoulder. The tide had come in, and Brad wanted to share it with me. We dangled our feet off the wall outside our hotel, listening to the waves. Those are moments to cherish, worth far more than Kay Jewelers will ever comprehend.

I celebrate another anniversary also precisely because of the painful times, those episodes that have periodically left us staring helplessly at a widening gulf between us. Years ago, in corporate life, I sat in a customer service seminar and learned an important truth. A company's most loyal customers are generally not those who have never had an issue with the product, but rather those who have experienced significant issues and the successful resolution of those issues. I can tell you without hesitation that the same truth applies to marriage. Late nights have found us immersed in deeply painful conversation, wounded by life or by each other, mists clouding the vision of eternity that should inspire us on. Sometimes we claw our way to the other side of the gulf, fingerhold by fingerhold. Sometimes we stumble on a miraculous bridge. But always, eventually, we find ourselves standing hand in hand on the far side of the impasse, a little bruised but stronger.

Brad forgives me. He inspires me, pushes me upward, expands my soul. He loves me at my most unlovable moments and believes I am beautiful. He honors me with honesty and gracefully accepts my honesty in return. He massages my feet even though he would rather not and stays up late at night so that I can wake up to a sparkling kitchen. He jumped into fatherhood without complaint, loving my son as his own. He is the champion of our children, even when they don't realize it, and my own safe haven when the storms swirl.

Simply put: I love my husband.

Chocolate, Cheese and Lessons from Little People
(September 2010)

Defenestration--as in "Mom, I saw a great picture of the Defenestration of Prague today"--is a great word. It doesn't slither off the tongue quite as deliciously as "plethora" or "thither," but it's still very nice. I should mention that the child describing defenestration (the act of throwing someone out of the window, by the way, in this case in political protest) is my 15-year old son. The same son apparently counts "extirpate" as one of his favorite words. I am ashamed to say I had to look that one up. I should, perhaps, worry that my teenager has his head filled with destruction, intellectually phrased or not. Given his ready wit and kind heart, however, I have decided in favor of amusement rather than horror.

I love that my sons have begun to embrace their inner nerdiness. My oldest son called from college this week, excited about his work in behavior analysis and describing the psychoanalytical theories of Anna Freud (Sigmund's daughter) with the same alacrity he used to display when describing a great snowboarding run in the powder of the Utah Rockies. These impromptu lessons in European history and child development are just the most recent of lessons I have learned from my children. I have learned a plethora (see, doesn't that slither nicely?) of lessons over the years at the feet of my offspring. The following are some of the highlights.

- The world has not created a food that cannot be improved by adding either chocolate or cheese. If chocolate won't fit the bill, cheese will. Trust me on this one. I have tried in vain to prove the theory wrong.

- Napoleon was not the last little person to rule an empire. Our 3 pound, 10 ounce daughter took the throne from her very first breath, and the age of the semi-benevolent dictator continues, four years later.

- A person who speaks with confidence can sound believable, even profound, even when he makes no sense whatsoever.

- Pajamas are world's most versatile fashion, acceptable for nearly any occasion, particularly school and particularly when worn with slippers in the middle of winter.

- Chill out. Relax through teenage driving adventures, surprise schedule changes, broken appliances, unexpected bills, bad hair days, and other calamities large and small. Listen to Bob Marley and remember that "every little thing is gonna be all right."

- A little computer time goes a long way. Alternatively, play games, cuddle, throw a frisbee, read silly stories, or dance. Your children, your husband, your dog, and your eyes will thank you.

- Wrinkled clothes and messy hair do not necessarily signify a flawed character.

- And finally, loving until your heart hurts may be more terrifying than bungee jumping, but it is also more wonderful than a million Lake Champlain chocolate truffles or even a lifetime pass to Disneyland.

Changing of the Guard

(October 2012)

Something about the ever-present cornfields here in central Illinois almost dares me to find them attractive, even now, when only stubble and dirt clods reach to the line of trees on the horizon. Oddly, despite my Rocky Mountain and Green Mountain roots, I do find myself irresistibly captivated by this agrarian sea that surrounds me. The city of Springfield offers less in the way of back country charm. Still, my drive home from work today brought me down wide, tree-lined avenues, signature scenery for the heartland. Here and there, trend-setting trees sported yellow and orange plumage, a sure sign that crisp autumn air waits just around the corner.

As I drove, I pondered how different life will look the next time I watch the trees trade their summer greenery for fall colors. This weekend, I will write to Devin on his mission and tell him about Alec's final Homecoming game. I might even confess that I teared up a bit when the senior float passed, carrying Alec and the other graduating football players.

I still picture Alec as a mischievous kindergartner, grinning gleefully as he tells how he and 10-year old Devin sneaked out onto the roof of the house during quiet time. Next autumn, the two brothers will drive off to college together, Devin a recently returned missionary and Alec a brand new adult. They will likely spend Sunday afternoons eating dinner with one set of grandparents or the other, building bonds and memories in a way their younger sister may not have the opportunity to enjoy a decade later when the grandparents approach their nineties.

The changing seasons seem to expose the mortality in all of us (at least those of us dancing around that mid-century mark). One cousin asked recently, "How did we get so old all of a sudden?" Another reminded me that my generation has become the aunts and uncles (and even grandparents!) that I remember so fondly from my school days. Back when those aunts and uncles still attended PTA meetings and sent children of their own off to college, I used to sing along to Bonnie Raitt's "Nick of Time":

> *I see my folks, they're getting old, I watch their bodies change*
> *I know they see the same in me, And it makes us both feel strange*
> *No matter how you tell yourself, It's what we all go through*
> *Those eyes are pretty hard to take when they're staring' back at you*
> *Scared you'll run out of time*

I loved the song then, knew all the words. Now I understand it in a way I never could in my twenties. The thought of getting old myself inspires no particular horror. But I raise my children here on the prairie, 1000 miles away from those aunts and uncles and parents who played such a pivotal role in my life. I find myself indeed scared I'll run out of time to share my extended family with my sons and daughter who know them primarily through long outdated stories.

See? Those corn-stubble vistas and colorful trees have me waxing nostalgic and feeling old. Pretty soon, winter will set in. I'll find a few more gray hairs, mark another milestone or two. But spring hovers in the wings even when the north wind sends frigid air down my neck. Nostalgia will have to give space eventually to rebirth and the blossom of new opportunity. The grandparents will once again trade their cross-country skis for hiking boots, and I will wake up to find that the world has not ended quite yet.

Home

(August 2010)

When I began to set up housekeeping on my own for the first time, I bought a set of blue willow dinnerware. I find the story behind the painted scene vaguely interesting, but the real reason I set my table with blue willow is because it reminds me of my grandparents' house. Every two years growing up, my family traveled cross-country from wherever we lived at the time to visit my grandparents in Cedar City, Utah. For Mother, these visits were "coming home" in the full sense of the word. Grandpa lived in his father's house, next door to the home where my mother grew up. Uncle Scott lived just past the garden, and the extended family still gathered at the piano to sing. Even with my own infrequent visits to Cedar City, I knew how the basement would smell and where to find my favorite books in the living room. And when I sat down to breakfast, I sat down to a table set with blue willow china.

Unlike my mother, I struggle when faced with the question "Where are you from?" or "Where do you call home?" Often, I simply take the easy way out and name whatever state happens to display on my driver's license. But every once in a while I look at those blue willow plates and wonder what "home" means for me.

I suppose for me home will never be a single place surrounded by walls and gardens, or even a single town with its collection of old friends and "remember whens." Rather, home is a collection of smells and sights and defining moments.

I see home in the rise of a full moon over the mountains, smell it in the heat rising off the cement on a mid-summer day or in the whiff of mountain pine in the early morning. I taste home when I make sugar muffins for my children on a Saturday morning or chocolate oatmealers for dessert. (My children call them no-bakes, but I secretly still call them "COs" in my mind, just as we did in my childhood.) I catch the scent of creosote on a railroad tie, and immediately I hear the long-ago chatter of cousins as we build my grandparents' cabin in Strawberry, Arizona. I grow roses to the side of the house, just as my mother did. I scribble notes in the margins of my books, stand for long minutes in front of a single painting in a museum, and in my mind my father stands at my side.

Ironically, given the fact that I have spent only 10 years of my life in the Southwest and given the fact that my political leanings make living there an exercise in patience, I find that any roots I have dig deeply into Rocky Mountain soil. When I go home in my head, I smell canyon air, I tell direction by the mountains, and I eat my dinner on blue willow china.

Preserving the Ideal: Mason Jar Memories

(August 2013)

For years I kept a dusty Mason jar, filled with home-bottled cherries, on my kitchen shelf. I have no idea how the jar arrived in my kitchen. I do know that I have never bottled cherries, and I know that my family would never eat the fruit. And yet, the jar presided over years of holiday meals and fresh bread, hurried breakfasts and midnight snacks. Perhaps I hoped that it would lend a sense of pioneer wholesomeness and a promise of home-cooked love that would settle over my family.

For me, personally, the cherries brought a touch of my childhood to my adult life. Growing up, canning season was a bustling reality at our house, following on the heels of gardening season. As autumn approached, Mother alternated between sewing our school clothes and minding the jars rumbling away in the canner on the stove. She bottled applesauce, pears, pickles, peaches, tomatoes, and whatever fruit was native to the area we called "home" that year. When our travels took us out West to visit family, we gathered cherries from the orchards in central Utah. I never liked the taste of the cherries as much as I liked the chunky applesauce and the bread and butter pickles, but I loved the way they looked with the rich burgundy of the cherry juice. And I loved the vacation memories they brought.

As my children grow older and my confidence in my nurturing skills dwindles, my own mother rises higher and higher on the pedestal of ideal motherhood. I struggle with the daily grind of cooking and remember family dinners and trays of fanciful holiday treats on New Year's Eve. I sigh impatiently when my younger children want to play a made-up game, and I remember Mother playing ball with me in the park and making a special tent to go over the card table. I explain to my teenager that I cannot possibly manage all of his activities along with my own, and I remember how Mother used to drive me across town for ballet three times a week.

I will never be the mother to my own children that my mother was to me, just as I will never eat that dusty bottle of cherries. But the ideal still presides over my kitchen thoughts and colors my dreams.

Making Friends

(August 2012—appears in the book *Florence Decker Corry: A Woman of Dignity, Charity and Grace*)

I have been making new friends these past few months. Charming people, really. Genuine, complex, lots of fun, inspirational. There's Florence, of course. I would love to grow up to be like her, if that's still possible at my age. I think most of all, I admire her ability to connect with people. Everyone gravitated to Florence, it seems. Her siblings returned to her home again and again to sit at her kitchen table and talk for hours. Her troubled nephew flagged her down on the highway once because he knew she would listen with compassion. The mentally handicapped man who sold spudnuts felt like he lost his best friend when she died. She held lawn parties and pajama parties. She inspired the youth that she taught. And she left a little of herself in each of her children.

Florence grew up in a trio of sisters along with Fae and Blanche, wonderful women in their own right. I knew Fae as an older woman but have enjoyed making the acquaintance of her younger self. She grew to womanhood in the 1920s, the granddaughter of pioneers. Her determination to write her own story inspires me, and I find myself indebted to her again and again for the volumes of history she left behind. She brought her parents and grandparents to life for me. We share an affinity for the national parks, it seems, and a tendency toward rebellion tempered by an overactive conscience.

Of the three sisters, I find Blanche's story the most poignant. As a young girl, she held her baby brother while he died and then grew up watching her mother fade away with tuberculosis. She pinned her life somewhere between the fragility of her mother and the stubborn strength of a father who both exasperated and enthralled her. Somewhere in that netherworld between the two, she lost herself. A fine writer with a soul that reached toward lofty heights, she often stumbled but still found beauty along the way.

The sisters shared a pioneer grandmother known for her spunk and formidable nature. Nancy Bean married and divorced twice before leaving one daughter behind and crossing the plains with her second daughter. She met my great-great grandfather upon his return from the gold fields of California, and the two joined the original settlers of Parowan, Utah. Nancy helped the women of the town birth their babies and clothed the men with her homespun suits, all while raising a dozen children. I'm not sure her pioneer spirit filtered down through the gene pool to me, but I love having this powerful woman in my ancestral line nonetheless.

I cannot pretend that I know exactly how this next life will shake out. I trust that the common vision of insipid angels singing endlessly with golden harps holds little semblance to reality. At least, I hope we have fashion choices in the eternities that reach beyond the formless white robe and unwieldy halo. I prefer to envision myself trading stories with Nancy while she teaches me how to weave or hiking with the trio of sisters through the mountains. Perhaps along the way we will encounter their father, Mahonri, with his beloved horses or Grandfather Zachariah target shooting with the pistol he called his "second wife." Until then, I will content myself with the joy of discovering my new friends through the memories of others and the shadows their lives left on my path.

A Moment Captured

(September 2011—appears in the book *Florence Decker Corry: A Woman of Dignity, Charity and Grace*)

I have a favorite picture of my grandmother, Florence. In the picture, a little girl with serious dark eyes and loose brown curls perches on a wrought iron chair. She looks slightly unsure, but not frightened, with perhaps the hint of a smile. Those same eyes, searching yet steady, show in photos of Florence as a teenager and a woman. Here, they gaze out over the chubby cheeks of a five-year old.

She clasps her hands lightly on the skirt of her white embroidery dress, a matching ribbon tied in a bow around her left wrist. She loved that dress, although looking back as an adult she thought the heavy black play shoes and dark stockings made for a hideous picture. Virgil loved the Sunday curls in her hair. Even moreso, he adored his half sister. Everyone loved Florence, from Virgil--home from college and about to get married--on down to the toddler, Woodrow.

Perhaps Florence, with her winning combination of determination and sweetness, reminded the family of all that was still good in a world gone wrong. With World War I in full swing, and brothers Virgil and Alvin waiting to be called up, even the sheltered Southern Utah town of Parowan needed the innocence of a cherub in white embroidery and black stockings.

And so Virgil whisked Florence to the town photographer to capture the beauty of Sunday curls and dainty dresses. Never mind the clunky shoes. Parowan finally boasted a town photographer, and children grew up all too soon in those days.

Florence herself met the world in short order. Three years passed in the warmth of summer rides on the hay wagon, evenings spent listening to Mamma (Harriet) reading poetry, and family singalongs at the organ. Then came what Florence later referred to, rather euphemistically, as "the Delta adventure." Father (Mahonri) sold their beautiful home and uprooted the family to Delta to seek their fortune. The business venture failed, and before the year was out, they returned to Parowan, penniless.

Delta claimed not only the family's pride but also the life of baby brother Homer. His death dealt a blow to Harriet's already frail health. Diagnosed with pulmonary tuberculosis while still in Delta, she willed her way through another eight years, finally dying in the middle of Florence's sophomore year of high school. The oldest child at home by this time, Florence shouldered much of the burden of those last years with her mother and essentially raised her younger brothers after Harriet's death.

The loss of her mother and the heaviness of the years after Delta left its mark on Florence and all of the children. But the warmth of those dark eyes prevailed. Inheriting her father's tenacity and her mother's grace, infused with her own remarkable compassion and capacity for joy, Florence never quite lost sight of the little girl in white with the steady gaze.

Romance, Corry Style

(October 2011)

Like many love stories, the story of Florence and Elwood begins with a date, Elwood's first. To be more precise, the story begins with basketball, hometown rivalry, and the wager of a box of candy. It was a Saturday night in January 1930. Cedar City's high school basketball team opened its season with a game against rival Parowan High School. Coach Linford's boys needed to prove themselves, and a win against a strong team like Parowan would set them on solid footing in their quest for the division championship. They had the home court advantage, and Elwood joined his friends to cheer on his team.

Elwood was a senior in high school and, despite a self-professed admiration for girls from about the third grade on, he had always felt too bashful to ask a girl on a date. As luck would have it, he found himself standing next to a Parowan girl during the game. They bantered about whose team would win, and Elwood jokingly said, "Well, I'll bet you a box of candy that Cedar wins." Cedar did win. Elwood forgot all about the bet.

A few days later, a box of candy arrived in the mail for Elwood with no return address. He puzzled over the origin of the candy for a few days before the light dawned. All of a sudden, he remembered the bet. He called the Parowan girl and asked her to go to a show and help him eat the box of candy. And that is the story of Elwood's first date with …Lillian Adams.

Wait! Lillian, you say? I thought this was a love story about Elwood and Florence. Ah, yes. Well, you see, Lillian and Florence were good friends, had been ever since they met in Miss Parry's 1st grade class. Lillian graduated a year early from high school and went to Cedar to start college while Florence finished her senior year at Parowan High. In Cedar, Lillian ran into Elwood at the aforementioned basketball game. They dated for a while until Elwood decided that perhaps he should avoid going too steady with any one girl before he served his two-year mission for the LDS Church.

In May of 1930, Elwood and Florence graduated from their respective high schools, and Florence joined her friend Lillian at the Branch Agricultural College (BAC) in Cedar City. Elwood knew her briefly before he left on his mission to England that October. In fact, he remembers seeing her one day as she walked toward campus and thinking, "I would like to ask that girl for a date sometime." Then missionary work filled his mind, and he forgot about Florence until he returned home from England.

The Christmas holidays of 1932 found Florence in the middle of her sophomore year at BAC. She lived with her sister Fae and kept busy with theater, student government, her sorority, and her work at Cedar Mercantile.

Far from Florence's thoughts, Elwood sailed home from England at the close of his mission, arriving home on Christmas Day 1932. Lillian, still rather enamored with Elwood, dragged Florence to church to hear Elwood's homecoming talk. Elwood makes no note of seeing her at his homecoming, but then the returned missionary's social calendar filled up pretty quickly in those first few weeks home.

In mid-January 1933, Elwood and Florence both found themselves at a party at the home of Bertha Seaman. Elwood arrived alone and saw Florence enter the room. She must have looked particularly striking that

evening, because he remembers thinking "here comes the bride" as he
watched her. Not realizing that Florence had come to the party as the date
of Waldo Adams, Elwood intended to ask her if he could take her home.
Either bashfulness or wisdom prevailed. In any event, Elwood left the party
alone.

A week or so later, the Cedar Second Ward planned an M.I.A. party. As he
hurried out the door to go somewhere with his friend C. J. Parry, Elwood
followed an impulse. "Wait," he called to C.J. "I have to go back in the
house for something." Back inside, he called Florence at her job at Cedar
Mercantile and made a date to take her to the party. Thus began a lengthy
courtship.

Planning a life together in the midst of the Great Depression often meant
delaying marriage for more practical matters. Elwood completed his
schooling at BAC and worked the family farm while Florence continued
working at Cedar Mercantile. He played tennis, competed on the debate
team, and served a term as Student Body President. She kept up with her
sorority, continued doing dramatic readings, and became involved with the
newly formed Business and Professional Women's Club.

While they waited to build sufficient finances for their marriage, Elwood
and Florence watched close friends get married. One of those friends was
Lillian Adams. In a speech she gave just months before her death, Florence
shared her admiration for Lillian for not letting the love triangle interrupt
their friendship.

As two years passed, day-to-day life and increasing responsibilities crowded
in. Florence and Elwood each supposed the other had begun to lose
interest in the relationship. In the summer of 1934, Elwood accepted a call
to serve as Leland Perry's counselor in the Second Ward bishopric. His
bishopric duties sometimes overshadowed romance. Florence recalled
sitting in the living room at the Corry home one evening, listening to cries
of "horsler" from the kitchen. Elwood had a bishopric meeting and needed
someone to take Florence home. In time-honored Corry tradition, the last
one to yell "horsler" pulled the short straw and played chauffeur.

But Elwood got a wake-up call one day from his friend Demoin, who
announced that Florence was dating someone else. As the story goes, she

even kissed the competition, a Swedish fellow named Roy Lundgren. Perhaps that was just the motivation Elwood needed.

Elwood's personal history mentions nothing about their courtship after the first date until an incident that occurred shortly before the wedding. It was June 1935, and Elwood was putting up hay on the farm with Rex Maxwell. Rex had no idea about the quickly approaching wedding until Elwood casually mentioned that he would be gone for a few days as he "had a little detail to take care of."

"What detail?" asked Rex.

"Oh, I'm getting married."

A bit put off by Elwood's casual approach, Rex raised his voice. "Man, you call that a little detail?" Elwood said Rex went on to lecture him about the importance of the step he was about to take. Apparently, he took the lecture to heart. In any case, the two married on June 21, 1935 in the St. George LDS Temple.

For Florence and Elwood, the real love story played out over the next 19 years of marriage. Together they weathered the financial devastation of the Great Depression, Elwood's service in World War II, and the deaths of their remaining parents. Together they raised a family of six children and built an insurance and real estate business. They supported one another in demanding church callings and community activities. And finally, after two decades of laughter and disappointment, hard work and good memories, they supported one another through Florence's final illness. While perhaps a little short on traditional romance, their romance, Corry style, has inspired generations of their posterity.

Nuclear Families

(March 2011—appears in the book *Florence Decker Corry: A Woman of Dignity, Charity and Grace*)

On May 19, 1953 the United States detonated a 32-kiloton atomic bomb (later nicknamed "Dirty Harry") at its nuclear testing facility in Nevada. With a blast three times the size of the Hiroshima bomb, Harry sent fallout drifting over a wide area, including Southern Utah. This was just one of over 100 bombs detonated above ground at the Nevada facility between 1951 and 1962 and one of five atomic bombs that had a fallout pattern covering Cedar City, Utah.

Isaac Nelson, a resident of Cedar City, describes taking his wife out to see the first explosion. It was dark, he says, just before daylight, "and we were chattering like chipmunks, so excited! Pretty soon, why, the whole sky just flared up in an orange-red flash, and it was so brilliant that you could easily see the trees ten miles across the valley, and if you had a newspaper you could have easily read it, it was so bright. . . ." Later, he says, town residents stood outside to watch the fallout clouds drifting up through Cedar. Isaac's wife died of brain cancer that developed shortly after one of those evenings spent watching the fallout cloud float by.

In a way, I grew up in the shadow of a nuclear cloud. A native of Cedar City, my mother was five years old when the nuclear testing began, and she tells stories similar to Mr. Nelson's. Thanks to cancer, she later donated both a breast and her thyroid to the American quest for adequate weaponry. My grandmother died of brain cancer just three years after the explosions began, leaving behind her a husband and six children. Though I have no proof that Harry or any of his atomic friends caused her cancer, medical reports of the period show brain tumors among the classes of cancer occurring in excess in the early period after nuclear testing.

My mother developed breast cancer about the time of my earliest memories, and she often spoke of her own mother's death from cancer. As children tend to color the world based on their own limited set of experiences and family stories, I then logically assumed that everyone contracts cancer at some point and saw that eventuality as a simple, if sad, fact of life. I accepted death with similar logic, aided by a religious perspective that emphasizes eternity. I never quite grew out of those assumptions.

Consequently, when my first husband's brain tumor returned from vacation with a vengeance, I recognized a pre-established pattern and quietly began planning for the inevitable. I know to some that view rings fatalistic, even regrettably morbid, and I suppose that if I saw death as an end--to self, to relationships, to progress--I would have to agree. As it happens, I see death more as a transition. With that in mind, our little family, each of us in our own time and fashion, began to plan for life on the other side of the approaching metamorphosis. Our son, just a toddler when his father died, absorbed and reflected his insulated world, blithely oblivious to the shock of innocent bystanders when he announced matter-of-factly that his daddy had died and was now in heaven.

I think of these patterns as the Fukushima Daiichi nuclear disaster unfolds in Japan. My Asian contemporaries grew up in a more striking nuclear shadow than I did. In August 1945, the United States dropped "Little Boy" and "Fat Man" on Hiroshima and Nagasaki. Two generations later, the nuclear pattern renews unexpectedly in the wake of an earthquake, once again fundamentally altering families with the fallout of power run amok.

Living a Meaningful Life

Searching for Zing
(October 2010)

We moved into a brand new house one year ago. Though three children and a dog have added their marks to doors, walls and counter tops, the house still feels new. The carpet shows exactly one spot of wear. It took me a while to realize the source of the worn circle next to the piano pedals, a circle that reappears no matter how often we vacuum the shag to attention. Then one day I watched Alec play piano, watched his heel push into the carpet as he worked the pedal. He ignores me when I stand and watch him play, absorbed as he is in his music. He leans into the keys, occasionally tapping the rhythm with his toe, and music fills the house.

In true teenage boy fashion, my son rarely discusses his stresses or elaborates about his worries. Instead, he plays the piano. He takes after my mother in this respect, and I envy them both. Childhood summers found me sitting in my grandfather's house, reading in the living room while Mother and a revolving collection of relatives created music around the piano in the side room. I remember gauzy curtains on the windows surrounding the piano, the scent of geraniums from the entranceway, and the murmur of voices figuring out parts or planning a violin obbligato. Those same voices rang out at family reunions and brought the Spirit rushing in at Grandpa's funeral. Heavenly choirs have nothing on the Corry family, except perhaps a touch of hushed reverence.

I used to dream of sitting at Grandpa's piano in an otherwise quiet house, running my fingers along the keys and sending my joy, my anguish or simply my moment of peace winging up Cedar Mountain by way of Chopin or Rachmaninoff. I never did learn how to filter my soul through my fingers. Periodically, I sit down to play a sonatina, sure that the emotion bubbling up inside of me will somehow guide the notes. Inevitably, I stumble on a chord, fracture an arpeggio, and eventually give up in disgust.

For a time, I hoped my voice could carry me where my fingers could not. I studied, practiced, sang concerts and funerals, even taught some wonderful students. I remember two times in particular when I caught a glimmer of the feeling I sought. In preparation for a master class, I finally gave in and learned a German art song full of emotion simmering just barely in control beneath the surface. With the master teacher's whispered coaching in my ear throughout the song, I felt the music and my soul click together for just a few moments. The music swelled, and my voice floated right along with it. I closed the piece, exhilarated by the experience.

Later, I sang in the sanctuary of a cathedral. Huge windows overlooked Lake Champlain, and the audience faded to insignificance in the expanse of wood, concrete and air. A friend had composed a gorgeous arrangement of a favorite spiritual for the occasion, and we joined with a talented oboist. Voice, piano, and oboe danced in and out of the haunting melody. Again, I felt the music and my soul combine.

I have not felt my voice and spirit click in many months, and I doubt I will feel that connection in the same way again. I have come to accept the fact that music is not my calling, though my soul responds to the talent of others. At the same time, this need to write has my fingers traveling keys again. I feel the tug of my soul reaching. More often now, the spirit inside me finds expression, and I feel the exhilarating click. The quest continues.

Warm Bread, Stolen Cookies and Other Life Essentials
(February 2011)

I have come to the conclusion that there must be a link between the stomach and the pen. Christopher Kimball, editor of *Cooks Illustrated* magazine, quickly rose to the top of my list of favorite essayists last year. Now, I find myself reading, quite by chance, a memoir of Ruth Reichl, the editor-in-chief of *Gourmet Magazine* up until its unexpected demise in 2009. Just a few chapters in, I am captivated by Ruth's rich stories (which she readily admits to embellishing, according to the time-honored tradition of her rather eccentric family). Ostensibly about her process of maturing into a full-blown foodie, the memoir reveals a rich understanding of the complexities and humor of human nature. Incidentally, it also includes a host of delicious recipes.

I suppose it makes sense, really, that foodies should have the ability to reach right to the heart of things. After all, isn't food the way to a man's heart? Don't we eat "soul food" and "comfort food"? Food provides a nostalgic link to our past and a hopeful path to our future, as in the cases of dieting or preparing a special meal for someone we desire to impress. We reward and punish with food. We eat or refuse to eat as a form of signalling confederacy or protest. Food figures prominently in our rituals and ceremonies, in our ethnic identity and our social gatherings. What, how, when, and with whom we eat offers a glimpse into our socio-economic status. And, in the end, we simply cannot survive without food.

My daughter had a birthday recently, her fifth. When I asked her for her birthday dinner menu, she responded with "bread and water for everyone...oh, and cake with ice cream." We did, indeed have bread for her birthday dinner: Portuguese sweet bread, fresh out of the oven and slathered with butter and either creamed honey or strawberry freezer jam. The sheer, glorious decadence of the thick slices of fragrant homemade bread differed rather sharply from the crust of bread and water we associate with prison food or even the unleavened bread the Savior portioned to his apostles at the Last Supper (although my daughter does regularly break her bread into small "sacrament" pieces). Isn't it odd how one simple menu can show such vastly different faces?

Though not quite as austere as a bread and water diet, I celebrated my move to Vermont some years ago by going vegetarian for a time. With its love of all things hippie and with a host of animal-friendly options, Vermont makes vegetarianism easy. For me, eating vegetables symbolized embracing my new life and complemented the process of healing after a long period of intense stress. Even the process of chopping copious quantities of squash and carrots for my favorite vegetarian chili grounded me, and the spicy scent of dinner simmering on the stove turned my small apartment into a home.

For many of us, in fact, food and home are practically synonymous. We taste a meatloaf just like Mom used to make or enjoy the liberty of refusing carrot and raisin salad even while fondly envisioning that very salad in its penguin bowl on our childhood dinner table. Like many families, my family builds traditions around special foods: Christmas lobster followed by steak with Bearnaise sauce (Dad makes the lobster and Mom makes the Bearnaise sauce), Irma's Kahlua cake for most birthdays, Devin's coffeecake for a Saturday morning treat, oatmeal bread dripping with swirled cinnamon for our friend Pat, pork fried rice in honor of Grandpa Larsen.

Another family tradition hearkens back to my college summer at a fishing resort on Alaska's Lake Iliamna. The lodge chef kept dozens of special recipe chocolate chip cookies in the walk-in freezer. The cookies made up part of the sack lunches for our guests to eat creekside, and employees were strictly forbidden to partake. Of course, we had strict orders against any number of temptations, and we felt unduly persecuted. Consequently, most of us gained a substantial number of pounds on stolen chocolate chip cookies. A laughing chef sent us home with the secret recipe at the end of the summer, and I have made the cookies for the past 20 years.

About the time I began and ended my life of cookie crime, Jeff Henderson decided to spend a portion of his prison sentence working in the kitchen. Incarcerated for drug dealing, he found a passion for cooking that carried him to executive chef positions in Las Vegas, a best-selling memoir, and a chance to give back. I find his story fascinating enough to recommend it. And I echo his philosophy that "food is a celebration of life, . . .that every recipe, every dish has a story behind it." I look forward to finding those stories, one spoonful at a time.

Milestones at the Middle

(March 2011)

Last month, I passed a milestone. It has now been five years and one month since I was last pregnant, a record amount of non-pregnancy time since I first began the motherhood adventure 21 years ago. I will never breastfeed again, never change my own baby's diaper, watch my own toddler take a shaky first step, or send my child to a first playdate. In a few months, my youngest child begins kindergarten. The young mother phase of my life will officially end. Never one to linger in one stage of life when another beckons, I watch its passing with little reluctance. Still, somehow I envisioned a rather more gradual transition from mommyhood to this pause in the shadow of approaching menopause.

Life travels on, marked milestone by milestone, and I find the changing landscape around me intriguing. I shuffle reading glasses on and off the bridge of my nose, not yet willing to commit to the bifocals I should wear. A once enviable metabolism disappeared long ago, and despite my unwavering commitment to regular exercise, an unflattering muffin top persists in spilling over the belt of my not quite in fashion jeans. My résumé, brimming with promise a decade ago, now sports a gigantic hole that would qualify me more for cleaning the office that once boasted my name on the door. I find myself more often in a mentoring role now, and the children I used to babysit have children in shoulder pads or scout uniforms. My own sister recently posted a picture of her fourth grandchild.

And yet...I have to agree with the old John Denver song that says "it turns me on to think of growing old." I do shudder at the thought of becoming decrepit, but I certainly have noticed an amount of sweetness in this ripening process brought on by a few years of experience. I suppose the fact that my parents have aged so well helps a great deal.

I realized a while back, to my pleasant surprise, that I no longer feel the need to win every race in life. My companions on the road look less like competition and more like inspiration. Their successes lift me up rather than reminding me of my failings, perhaps because life has made me acquainted with myself. While I still challenge myself, still push my comfort zone and reach for my personal best, I have come to understand my own rhythms and how to let those rhythms propel me forward.

As I leave toddler dreams behind, I find myself growing with my children. I love mothering older children, watching their personalities emerge and sharing their excitement as the world expands in front of them. I also love contemplating with my husband the not-so-distant-as-it-used-to-be possibility of an expanding world of our own. While this middle phase of life finds me vaguely adrift, searching for a path and just the right answer to the eternal question of "what shall I be when I grow up," I like the view from here, with my fingers trailing in the water and the stars all around. Life holds promise, and I have time.

Happy Scars

(June 2011)

I am building a new crop of scars as I write--a half moon on my inside left calf, with a series of oozing constellations mirrored on both legs. Poison ivy designed the scene, aided and abetted by my eventual inability to resist the overwhelming urge to apply long fingernails to the blisters. I have rarely felt anything as glorious as those brief seconds of relief from the infernal itching! Besides, since I encountered the ivy to begin with in the midst of an absolutely perfect family vacation, I can hardly complain. I scar easily, it seems, and the scars leave a map of my life on my skin, prompting memories, odd snapshots of random moments frozen in time.

Not far from the emerging constellations rests the scar of a small hole in my shin. I was five, running down the street with my friend Jenny in Vermilion, South Dakota. Jenny was my first best friend, and we played together whenever our mothers met for church functions. That day, while our mothers chatted or baked bread or planned some now long-forgotten event, we took Jenny's little sister for a dash in her stroller. The stroller hit a bump, stopped dead, and up in the air I flew, only to land quite precisely on a small, pointy rock. Jenny moved a year or two later, but I think of her now and again and wonder what sidewalks she has jogged since that 1970s summer afternoon.

My ring finger sports a battle scar from a round lost to a small pot of startlingly hot tea water. College summers found me working in some of America's most beautiful vacation spots. I cooked Rocky Mountain oysters for drunken lodge guests near Yellowstone, brewed endless pots of coffee to welcome wealthy fisherfolk to the brilliance of early June mornings in the Alaskan bush, and served tea to the more sedate guests at a Vermont country inn on the lakeshore. Truth be told, I was a rather terrible waitress. Still, I loved the scenery and the people I met. On misty mornings, Brenda and I brewed our own steaming cups of herb tea and settled into Adirondack chairs on the wide porch to contemplate the waves lapping the beach and the splendid freedom of the early blush of adult life.

Other scars tell perfectly mundane stories of trays of chocolate chip cookies placed a little too close to the top rack of the oven or the new (to us) television Brad and I carried up a flight of stairs. Only a few scars, like the white cross on my forehead, bring the memory of pain. The rest remind me of a rich life filled with the laughter of family game nights, breathtaking discoveries of beauty, and the warmth of friendships. I thank God for the sweet memories, made all the sweeter by lessons of the white cross.

Living a Life of Passion

(February 2012)

A college friend of mine pasted a peace symbol on the top of his mortar board at our graduation. I scoffed to myself at his attempt to borrow the trappings of a previous era to play the intellectual rebel. After all, we graduated on a sunny spring day in the late 1980s in northern Utah. The Vietnam War had ended long ago, and those of us outside of international politics hadn't begun to think about the Gulf War. Even the Cold War had begun its closing scenes. We were middle-class white kids on a college campus not exactly famous for a diverse population. We had little to protest.

I have gained a greater respect for my peace sign friend over the years. He was passionate. He believed firmly in justice. A respected photojournalist, he has spent his career giving form and color to the ideals he used to spout over a bottle of Chianti. I wonder if I have succeeded as well in my own ideals.

I drew my first breath in Cache Valley, the rather idyllic little valley that also formed the backdrop for my college years (though life took me on a bit of a journey between infancy and freshman year). On the day I was born, far from my Rocky Mountains, the United States bombed Hanoi for the first time, two years after the Americans joined the ground war in Vietnam. Back in the States, Mohammad Ali officially announced that he would not submit to the draft. As he said, "I ain't got no quarrel with them Viet Cong...No Viet Cong ever called me nigger." Widespread war and race protests were just around the corner, and Ali's stand helped feed the growing flames.

About the time I broke out into my first baby smile, my family moved to Eugene, Oregon so that my father could complete his doctorate. He studied romantic poets and drank in the protest movement then thriving on the

University of Oregon campus. He, too, has lived a life of passion and ideals. As an educator, he championed the arts and highlighted regional history and culture. Privately, he addresses injustice one wounded soul at a time.

I think of my father's integrity in living according to his vision of the world as it should be. I think of my college friend and his peace sign, of Muhammad Ali and his stand against the war. All three live according to a driving force, and I admire that. To an extent, I tend to measure success by how people use their gifts and their life experiences to benefit others. By that measure, my parents rank among the most successful people I know. By that same measure, I fall short.

Now, having fallen short, I think it's time for me to fix my gaze upward and outward and start climbing.

Pinning My Dreams

(March 2012)

Recently, lulled by an hour of boredom on a windy afternoon, I gave in to peer pressure and created an account on Pinterest, the virtual bulletin board through which folks trade craft ideas, recipes, and dreams. I initially avoided the site because I abhor crafting. I peeked in the door because I needed a good hummus recipe. I pulled up a chair because I rediscovered dreaming.

I used to dream. Long ago and far away, in a small town in South Dakota, my father had an office in our basement. In that office, he created bookshelves out of cement blocks and long plywood boards. Yellow magazines lined those shelves, marching along in a most orderly fashion according to their publication date. For years, my parents subscribed to *National Geographic* magazine, and they kept every edition. Every once in a while, perhaps on a Sunday afternoon, we would go on a trip.

"Where do you want to go today?" my parents would ask.

"Hmm...China sounds good," I would answer. Or maybe Alaska, or Egypt, Antarctica.

And off we went. We combed through indices for articles, gathered stacks of magazines, and began our journey, photograph by photograph.

We packed those yellow magazines in the back of a UHaul before long and drove off on a real adventure to the Deep South. Two years later we moved again, then again. Eventually, we replaced the cement blocks with real bookshelves, the magazines with Google.

In the freedom of early adulthood, I lived a few of my dreams. After all, at nineteen or twenty-something, roadblocks cease to exist. I wanted to hike in the Grand Tetons, so on my day off one summer I stuck out my thumb and hitched a ride. I dreamed of Alaskan tundra, so I found a job and hopped on a plane. Later, I ached for fresh horizons and cozy New England villages with covered bridges and white steeples. This time, I packed my own UHaul and shared the dream with my young son.

That young son grew up, as did his brothers and sister. Our small apartment gave way to a house and piles of things. I built and buried a career. Life happened. I reveled in Christmas snows, sobbed at petty betrayals, gloried in mountaintop views, but I forgot to dream of faraway places.

And then, I gave in to peer pressure and pulled out the thumbtacks. My "Recipes" bulletin board looked lonely, so I added "Favorite Books" and then "Favorite Places." The photos of dreams realized reminded me of dreams set aside--dreams of Norwegian fjords, European cathedrals and national parks still unvisited. It seems the more I give vision to my dreams, the more capacity I find to dream, and those dreams in turn bring the lightness of possibility to life here and now.

If you promise not to tell, I will confess a momentary gratitude for peer pressure and silly social media.

Resting Between Sets

(February 2013)

I have spent my life with my eyes fixed on one goal or another, checking items off a myriad of lists line by line along the way. Those checks help me round out my sense of self, and the lure of unknown wonders around the next bend pulls me forward. I earned a degree, built a career or two, completed projects, lost the baby weight (finally), hiked mountains and conquered fears. Ah, but those milestones on the road to wonderful feel good!

Every once in a while, my current crop of goals grows stale. Life moves on to the next phase, and I find I require a new rhythm, new purpose. I study, ponder, try to match my heartbeat with the divine. Such was the case last fall, and over a few months I reached some surprising conclusions. Step back. Read. Breathe. Live in the present. Learn to radiate joy. And the hard one: defy logic and set aside the lofty goals for a time.

I embraced the plan initially. Learning to find joy, to accept life without the constant fight to make it fit my plan, felt incredibly liberating.

And then I stepped out of a rare mid-day bubble bath one afternoon and looked in the mirror in a moment of hormone-inspired introspective clarity. (Women, you know those moments.) "What a load of hooey!" I thought (in roughly those terms). "I have simply lowered my expectations of myself, of life. I have given up in defeat, thrown away the dream. I have become the lazy servant with his talent buried firmly in the sand." The thought pattern continued on with a fair amount of ranting and raving and glum expression, but that's pretty much the general theme. A quiet voice in a far corner of my brain reminded me that I had arrived at this path deliberately and under inspiration, but louder arguments drowned it out.

Winnie the Pooh has his favorite "Thotful Spot," a place made for "deciding what to do today." I have my own favorite thoughtful spots, and after a day of ranting and wallowing, I went to one of them. My mind wandered to one of my recurring goals that has impacted my life significantly over the past decade. I exercise religiously, and several days each week my regimen involves weight training. I love feeling strong, and I love the curve of a solid muscle. I thought about how those muscles grow. In simple terms, under the stress of pushing weight, the muscle tissue breaks down. It is in the recovery period (the rest in between sets, the good night of sleep) that the muscle rebuilds and grows.

Uncomfortable as it is to learn to define myself without the measuring stick of goals and accomplishments, this time of recovery is critical, and it will not last. This is a time to build strength and patience, to gather wisdom and grow faith. This is a time to hone insights, to cement good physical and spiritual habits, to nurture relationships. I still have a work to do, mountains to climb, loads to carry. Soon it will be time for the next set of reps, and I will need all of that strength and faith and insight when the time comes. For now, I will breathe, read, smile...and grow.

Mutterings from the Cesspool of Reality

(May 2013)

I find I don't mind middle age so much. I like the freedom that comes with children growing older. I like that we middle folks find it easier to toss aside the facade than we used to, that we seem to have grown more comfortable with the definition we have evolved for ourselves. I feel strong, involved (when I want to be), aware of connections in life around me in a way that I could not have been as a younger woman.

What gives me less joy is the fact that somehow in these middle years we give in to reality. We mature, we apply our experience to our vision of life. We work through our relationships and share our epiphanies with our friends who also struggle with making sense of their own lives. The challenges of raising children and growing a marriage hit us broadside in these middle years, more often than not, and sometimes we reel from the blow. Like most folks, I find a measure of comfort in realizing that my marriage is actually better than most, that the struggles we occasionally face as a family barely hit the Trials and Tribuations charts.

And yet, as I talk with friends and family, as I read blogs and even celebrity interviews, it seems that in our wisdom and maturity we give up on our dreams. Most kids fall way short of the brilliance promised in the proverbial Christmas letter. All marriages struggle. Gwyneth Paltrow reflected the collective middle-age marital wisdom in an interview recently. In that interview, she reported that her father said once that he and his wife have stayed together all these years because they never both wanted to get divorced at the same time. The reality is that most couples fight at least occasionally. The reality is that most professionals fail to find deep satisfaction in their careers. The reality is that few people reach the dreams that propelled them forward in their 20s.

Well, you know what? Reality stinks. The fact is that my dreams *did* propel me forward. Reality carries nothing even akin to the motivating power of dreams. In fact, comforting as it may be in a low moment to realize that my failure to reach that far away star simply means I join the rest of humanity on the ground, I happen to like the stars. The view from the lofty heights (or even the view on the way up to the lofty heights I may never reach) awes and inspires me way more than the view from the stable rocks and well-worn dusty paths of reality.

So thank you very much for the wisdom and the camaraderie here on the ground. I appreciate the clarity, and I see the logic. Truly I do. But until I hit another low point, I think I'm going to go back to assuming that the universe has something grand in store if I can only fly high enough.

Moonlight Magic

(September 2013)

I greeted a friend last night and noted the weariness apparent in her face. Her eyes mirrored the expression in so many faces I see. Perhaps autumn catches us all a little off our game with the abrupt switch from the delightful chaos of summer to the post-vacation structure of papers to sign, appointments to keep, children to motivate. Perhaps this friend, like so many of us, navigates a period of transition.

In a couple of hours, another friend enters the hospital for surgery and the beginning of treatment for breast cancer. She wonders if she will find the strength and the courage she needs. I know she will. My oldest son adjusts to life after a two year religious mission, reminding himself how to negotiate finances and dating, while his brother prepares to enter the mission field and give up the world for a time. One cousin finishes a college degree in mid-life, while another battles cancer and contemplates graduating from life a little early. Meanwhile, I bike through falling leaves, and the wind carries a chill from the north. The seasons are changing.

This year feels momentous for me. It isn't really, in the eternal scheme of things. We have our own family transitions, with half of the children living on their own now and the two at home growing so quickly. And yet, we still get up every morning, drink our kale smoothies for breakfast, send the children off to school, go to work, wonder how we will pay the bills even though we know the money always comes through in the end. The sun rises and sets. The farmer will harvest the corn outside my window soon and then plant again in the spring, as he does every year.

Perhaps this year feels momentous because I want it to be, because I believe it has the possibility of sparkle and depth. Some days, many days, I feel the weariness I saw on my friend's face last night. Today I feel oddly powerful as I sit in my office in my workout clothes, procrastinating exercise and listening to my dog snore on the floor at my feet.

For me, the new year begins with the close of summer. This year the close of summer found me in the Wyoming Rockies while I crossed "hike the Wind Rivers" off my bucket list. My adult boys and I spent a few perfect days hiking, philosophizing, and soaking up beauty in the Green River Lakes region. In the evenings, I watched the moon rise over the mountains while I stirred the fire. For me, Rocky Mountain moonrises hold a special magic, the promise of adventure. They carried me into adulthood my first summer away from home and presided over my farewell when I headed East for a new life. I can see clearly in my memory the progress of the moon over the mountaintop, teetering on the edge for strength before launching into the sky.

Obviously, the moon holds no inherent magic, whether it rises over the Rockies or over a Midwestern cornfield. But perhaps, if I work hard enough to let that moonlight shine through this change of seasons and into the next, I can bring the magic in. I can write more, pull myself out of a rut and into a rhythm, reach higher, breathe more deeply, soak in more of the beauty that surrounds me. I can make the year momentous.

Cologne, Confessions and Opportunity Cost

(October 2013)

I know it's a bit retro, in a 1980s mullet kind of way, but I have to admit that I still think cologne is kind of sexy. I don't mean Axe body spray, and I don't mean Old Spice (even though the commercials make me chuckle). I mean good, old-fashioned cologne, the kind we used to buy our boyfriends for Christmas in college, back in the long ago day. I even miss wearing a little Estée Lauder myself. My husband bought me an Egyptian musk a while back, and he tells me it smells wonderful, but apparently it fits my biology perfectly, because once it hits my skin, I smell nothing. That's how it should be, of course, and I even hesitate to wear the musk very often, so as to avoid offending the olfactory sensitivities of my allergic friends. Still, I miss the lovely dose of nostalgia that comes with an unexpected scent on the air. Sigh. I miss peanuts on airplanes, too. I'm such a cretin.

Since I started along this confession path, I may as well get it all out there.

I miss swearing with abandon. Yes, I still swear, but I do apply a filter much more frequently than I used to. They say that profanity is a sign of a small vocabulary. That may be, but you would be amazed at how creative a literate person can wax with a few well-chosen four-letter words. Did you know, for instance, that many expletives can morph into almost any part of speech (noun, verb, adjective, adverb...)? I can thank my college education for that little gem of knowledge.

I miss wasting time on a regular basis. I freely admit that I still manage to lose a few hours to blogs and Facebook on occasion, but I feel guilty about it every time. I remember spending whole days wandering Cache Valley in search of, well, nothing really. And I remember watching late night TV or talking until dawn. These days, I sneak in a nap or a chapter of a book and then kick myself for the items I could have checked off my "to do" list instead. Blast that stupid list!

I miss partying. Oh, don't have a conniption. I never drank, never felt the need to drink. But I do miss being able to let go, to dance without worrying about how silly I look. I miss late night philosophical discussions, half in Spanish and half in English, on the front stoop under the stars, with music drifting through the screen door behind me. I hardly admit to knowing any Spanish these days, afraid someone will expect me to speak, and I will make a fool of myself.

I recognize, with some heaviness, the opportunity cost of decisions I made long ago with much deliberation. I chose adventure over home, and now I begin to realize how little I know my extended family and how amazing these people are who share my heritage. In another sense, I chose home over career, and even after more than a decade away from the office, I struggle to find my sense of self without the projects and accolades. In either case, I would make the same decision all over again, but I sense the cost of those decisions more than I once did.

I find I do not mind the sense of loss too much. As long as I avoid getting stuck in the memory, a little backward glance now and again reminds me just how rich and full my life has been over the years and hints at the possibilities ahead. I don't imagine the coming years will find me hitchhiking in Yellowstone again, but the memory of my Yellowstone summer prods me to stick my metaphorical thumb out and see what surprises life has to offer down an unknown path or two.

Living with Dignity

(November 2014)

This past weekend, two women faced death. Both women had been diagnosed with incurable brain cancer. Both were young, beautiful, vibrant, with loving families and the world at their feet. Both chose to spend the remaining months of their life fighting for something bigger than themselves. For many, these women stand out as courageous examples of heroism.

On New Year's Day 2014, Brittany Maynard received a staggering diagnosis. 29 and recently married, she now contemplated brain cancer. Surgery proved ineffective, and by April doctors told her the tumor had grown into a grade 4 glioblastoma, an aggressive cancer that would likely claim her life within six months. Brittany and her family researched the options, none of them pretty. Treatment could prolong her life but not save it, and the side effects of the treatments themselves would drastically reduce the quality of what little time she had left. The tumor already promised a terrifying decline. Adding side effects of radiation and chemotherapy seemed unpalatable.

Have watched a loved one die from a grade 4 glioblastoma, I claim some experience with the indignity of the death the disease inflicts. I have watched a once handsome and athletic body grow puffy and weak with steroids. I have wept with frustration as the honor student struggled to pass classes that once came easily to him and finally struggled even to remember how to tie his tie. I held his hand as he recovered from yet another seizure, and I injected morphine to control the awful pain. I fought with insurance companies, propped a bowl under his chin while he threw up blood, and talked long into the night with him about what it might feel like to leave this life. In the end, I changed the diaper of a man who no longer recognized me. No one deserves to die that way.

While Brittany struggled with her own illness, another young woman also contemplated a diagnosis of terminal brain cancer. Lauren Hill, a high school senior and standout basketball player, had just signed on to play basketball for Mount Saint Joseph University in Cincinnati when she was diagnosed with Diffuse Intrinsic Pontine Glioma (DIPG), a rare form of brain cancer. 90% of children with DIPG die within 18 months of diagnosis. Like a glioblastoma, this cancer offers no pity to its victims.

Brittany and Lauren both took their fight to the next level, although they chose very different paths. Brittany began to research "death with dignity," or physician-assisted suicide, hoping to die on her own terms and spare her family the pain of watching her decline. She lived her last months deliberately, cherishing time with loved ones and building memories. At the same time, she joined forces with Compassion & Choices, an end-of-life nonprofit advocacy organization, to share her story, one that has sparked a national debate. She allowed herself to be vilified by those who disagreed with her choice, feeling that her cause was worth the cost. She ended her life on November 1, surrounded by love and still in control.

The day after Brittany's death, Lauren Hill played her first college basketball game. Mount Saint Joseph games usually draw a crowd of 50 people. For this game, 10,000 tickets sold out in 30 minutes. Lauren had chosen to spend her final months raising awareness of DIPG, in the hopes that increased research could help those who come after her, children and families who need a voice. In the months leading up to that November game, she practiced with her teammates and worked tirelessly for the cause that hit so close to home, all while undergoing painful treatments and suffering the debilitating effects of her disease. In the opening seconds of the game, she scored the first basket of the NCAA season, and the crowd erupted into cheers. Doctors say Lauren has weeks left to live.

I have thought a great deal this week about these two women. I find Lauren's story incredibly inspiring, much moreso than Brittany's, if I have to be honest about it. Fighting to the end always makes for a better story, especially when that fight includes two basketball teams and 10,000 fans coming together to make a dream come true for a girl who has decided to use her last weeks to help make possible the dreams of other children. One would have to be heartless, indeed, to find fault with Lauren and her end-of-life choices.

At the same time, I cannot quite bring myself to condemn Brittany. While I have watched a loved one suffer the agony of death, I have not personally felt the pain, the nausea, the terror, the disorientation, the loss of mental and emotional competence that comes with an illness such as hers. After 9/11 I told myself I probably would have jumped from the tower rather than allow myself to suffer death by fire. And I tell my husband that if I ever face severe dementia, I want to die alone in a nursing home rather than have my family see me in such a decline (although I have a feeling I would change my mind if that scenario ever became my reality). Is that really any different than Brittany taking a lethal dose of barbiturates only weeks or even days before the cancer would have claimed her life anyway?

I know so little about death. But one truth I have learned is that regardless of how many loved ones or journalists surround us, we each face the end privately, in the quiet moments of faith or fear, in the contemplation of our lives behind us and the possibilities ahead, or simply in the day to day struggle with illness and pain. Most of us get no rehearsal for our meeting with death, so it's game on when he turns his attention to us. We cannot with any certainty know how we will react or what path we will take, so perhaps we should spend a little less time condemning the end-of-life choices of others and a little more time following Lauren's example by living with dignity.

When asked what her daughter's epitaph might say, Lisa Hill responded with, "She never gave up, not even for a moment. She never strayed from her goals. She lived and loved with passion and desire." That is how one lives with dignity. Death will take care of itself.

Connecting with the Heavens

Thinking About Eve

(September 2010)

I have been thinking about Mother Eve today, not fully understanding her complex character or the complicated role she played. In some settings, we revere her. More often, we think of a rather foolish (or at least innocent and gullible) Eve giving in to the slick reasoning of a silver-tongued serpent. She effectively introduced transgression into the world and dragged poor Adam down a path that led them from idyllic garden to weed patch.

I like to think of Eve as forward-thinking rather than foolish. Even with limited, pre-apple vision, she seemed to realize the apparent contradiction between the warning not to partake of the fruit and the commandment to bear children. God had, after all, given Adam and Eve the fruit that he told them not to eat, and the garden state made the bearing of children impossible.

Eve transgressed, to be sure. She heard something in the serpent's arguments that sounded logical enough to convince her to put aside God's warning. Adam, wise in recognizing either the inevitability of the situation or the foresight of his wife, followed suit. They shared an "oops, we messed up" moment, hid, confessed, learned a critical lesson, took their consequence without complaint, and made life possible for all of us.

I have had some experiences lately that bring me, in a small way, a greater understanding of Eve. I tend to prefer action to lengthy contemplation, forward movement to stasis. While a host of miss-steps have taught me to pause and ponder a bit before acting, I still find myself all too often leaping out into the abyss without a clear notion of my landing spot. I open my mouth when wise women would keep silent.

Most recently, last week I made yet another error in judgment. I offended at least one person deeply, caused a dear friend a great deal of stress, and generally created a mess. I made the error thoughtfully, though, with a pretty good knowledge of the risks. In the end, a number of us learned valuable lessons that will benefit us down the road, lessons not so easily learned without the aforementioned mess.

This minor experience comes after a period of contemplating huge breakthroughs in my personal life gained only after several years of pain and messiness initiated in good part by my calculated disregard of some wise advice. I have concluded that the gain far outweighs the rather significant cost exacted. Life is like that.

Please understand. I do not presume myself or my experiences equal to Eve. However, I have come to realize that some of the important lessons and growth in life involved some either brave or foolish soul making a mess and seeing it through. Hopefully, as I think likely with Eve, the mess is perfectly suited to the divine end. Often, at least in my own life, God helps us spin gold out of the straw we spilled all over the floor. In any case, I owe my existence to Eve's willingness to risk her own life (not to mention garden bliss) for me.

City on a Hill
(November 2010)

When my husband came to Springfield on a house-hunting trip last year, he asked for directions to the church. "Just look for the power plant, and that's your exit," they said. Directions like that make even Vermont directions sound as specific as a chemical formula. I rolled my eyes and chuckled...until I saw the power plant. Accustomed to locating myself in relation to mountains, I find this flat farmland a little disconcerting. Fortunately for me, Springfield had the foresight to build a monstrosity of a power plant with huge smokestacks, visible from 20 miles away. As long as I can see those smokestacks, I know where I am.

While I appreciate the visibility of the smokestacks in Illinois or Mount Mansfield in Vermont, I have not always appreciated my own visibility. As a teenager, I hated my mother's lectures about example. "People watch you," she said, generally in relation to the modesty of my clothes (or the, um, occasional lack of modesty), my language, or how I treated others. Particularly as I left home for college, I fought against the pressure of expectation, hoping to relax and explore my boundaries. My personality never required a full-scale rebellious phase, but away from home my skirts slipped higher up my leg and my language descended rather closer to the gutter. I lived my religion faithfully, but that fact always surprised folks who knew me only casually. Their surprise brought my mother's voice to mind. "Avoid the appearance of evil." Bleah.

Twenty-five years later, I find myself reminding my teenage son that he is both cursed and blessed with visibility. With his confidence, his intelligence, and his engaging personality, he draws attention whether he likes it or not. "You and I do not have the option of anonymity," I tell him. Hopefully, he recognizes both the opportunity and the responsibility of being visible.

The Savior taught his disciples that a city set on a hill cannot be hid, reminding them of their responsibility to shine a light to lead the world to good things. I am sure Peter would have preferred to fade into the crowd outside the palace of Caiaphas, but his devotion to the Savior and his impetuous nature made that impossible. Peter rose to the challenge of example, though not always gracefully. In that messy process of learning to shine, he set a powerful, yet humble, example of discipleship.

The Gardener

(April 2011)

For me, the most powerful image of Easter is an intimate garden scene. The crosses that towered on Golgotha under threatening skies two days before stand empty now, though the memory of blood and agony casts a shadow over flowers opening in the early morning sun. Mary stands outside the empty tomb, weeping, puzzled at the words of the angels, who proclaim, "He is risen." Her hands, carrying spices to anoint the body of her master, fall useless to her side. She does not understand, can only wonder while she lets the tears flow.

Turning, she sees a man standing before her. Perhaps tears cloud her vision. In her distraction, she sees only a gardener. "Sir, if thou have borne him hence, tell me where thou hast laid him, and I will take him away."

"Mary."

Just one word turns anguish to joy, despair to hope. For Mary, for the world, light has pierced the darkness. No angel choirs herald the event. No cheering crowds shout hosannas. One woman kneels at the Savior's feet in awe and joy and whispers, "Rabboni."

I have not touched the scars on those feet, and I can scarcely imagine the tenderness of the exchange on that resurrection morning. And yet, I have sometimes felt the Savior call my name, His voice gently wiping away the tears and doubt. I have had no visions on the road to Damascus, just a multitude of answered prayers, of unexpected rainbows and slightly dusty angels bringing "I love you" notes from the master gardener.

Waiting for the Call

(April 2011)

My son called yesterday to say that his mission call is in the mail. In a few short days, a white envelope will arrive to tell us where Devin will spend the next two years of his life. I will, of course, resist the powerful temptation to steam open the envelope, only to fake surprise later when we open the call together as a family. The transformative process leading up to this mission call has been powerful, and this is Devin's door to open.

In a way, I envy my son the certainty of a calling. It has been some time since I could claim any certainty about my "mission in life." When hiking, I relish the opportunity to wander aimlessly for a while, admiring the flowers and the view along the way. In life, however, aimless wandering soon leaves me restless, searching for the magnetic pull of a purpose. Amory Blaine, whose coming of age Fitzgerald chronicles in *This Side of Paradise*, reaches the far side of a period of disillusionment to discover a general sense of his purpose. The narrator explains:

> *"He found something that he wanted, had always wanted and would always want--not to be admired, as he had feared; not to be loved, as he had made himself believe; but to be necessary to people, to be indispensable."*

I learned long ago that no one is indispensable. However, that desire to be necessary resonates with me. For me, the need goes a bit further. I want to be necessary to people, but also to God. I crave the feeling that the universe somehow needs me. I like the idea of the interconnectedness of life. For instance, I find it fascinating that for one in every five breaths I take I owe a debt of gratitude to Prochlorococcus, an oceanic microbe that no one even knew existed until 1986. More powerful is the philosophy that all human experience is intertwined: the present linked to the past and to the future, individual lives all dependent on the weaving that binds disparate threads into complex patterns.

Still, demanding soul that I am, I want more. I want to know specifically how I can lift my corner of the universe. Long ago, I pledged to consecrate all that I am and have to God. It is a lofty pledge, noble...and sometimes rather vague. I find myself looking for a blueprint. Even a scrap of paper with a quick note will do, like the ones I tack on the fridge for my own children. "Dear daughter, I need you to spiff up that tiny spot in the corner over there. Use that cleaning bucket of talents I gave you--the blue one this time--and make it sparkle."

For whatever reason, God seems generally loath to hand out the task and the tools at the same time. Either he gives us a task and leaves us to figure out a plan of attack, or he helps us find our set of tools and talents and then leaves us to figure out a use for them.

Today I pondered this notion of consecration. I have found that when I give in to impatience and try to design my own calling, I invariably spin my wheels. I gain greater traction when I throw my effort into finding and developing my talents, sharpening the tools. If I listen hard and exercise what little patience I possess, eventually something nudges me down the right path. Perhaps the trick to consecration, then, sometimes rests in consecrating the desire to serve. Perhaps if I do that and stop obsessively checking my cosmic mailbox every day for a call, I will in time find myself serving in meaningful ways.

Corrective Lenses

(April 2011)

While studying the other day, I chanced across the following scripture in the *Book of Mormon*: "But a seer can know of things which are past, and also of things which are to come, and by *them* shall all things be revealed, or, rather, shall secret things be made manifest, ... and also things shall be made known by *them* which otherwise could not be known." (Mosiah 8:17, italics added for emphasis)

I have always assumed that "them" in the scripture refers to "seer," and that is probably correct. Grammatically, however, "them" more logically refers to "things which are past" and "things which are to come." Now that set me to musing. Given the seer's role in correctly interpreting the past and future, I do not think my musings are entirely inappropriate. That said, with all due apologies to seers living and dead, I am not going to chat much about them today. Instead, I have been thinking in more basic and personal terms about the importance of viewing the present through the corrective lenses of the past and the future.

A talk in the LDS General Conference this past weekend reminded me of the story of Aron Ralston. The movie *127 Hours*, released last fall, brought Ralston's story to prominence again, seven years after the hiker saved himself by amputating his own arm while solo hiking in a remote canyon in Utah. I knew the general story but had not heard Ralston's account of a vision that he credits with giving him the motivation to proceed with his nearly impossible task. Dying of starvation and thirst, his arm pinned under an 800 pound boulder for five days, Ralston carved his epitaph into the rock, filmed his last words to his family and waited to die. Delirious with the ordeal by this point, he describes the scene:

> *"I was at peace with the idea of me dying. But then I saw this vision of this little boy and it shifted me, it gave me hope to get out because this is my future son, I could see me interacting with him without my hand at some point many years down the road and I realized if I'm going to have that son then I have to get out of here, I WILL get out of here, it got me through that last night..."* (quoted from an interview in 2010)

Aron Ralston's vision of things which are to come changed his view of his present circumstances, pushed him beyond his own natural capabilities. We may never have to saw away at our own arms to save our lives, but we do have opportunities in life to endure daunting trials, or even to relinquish an arm of sin, if you will. Our vision of the future, be it an eternity with loved ones or a more immediate promise of desired blessings, can give us the perspective shift we need to press forward.

Likewise, a thoughtful examination of the past (in contrast with an obsessive dwelling on remembered offenses or triumphs) can also unearth hidden pearls of wisdom applicable to present trials or conundrums. Some time ago, I received what felt like an inspiration or a premonition. It was an odd premonition, and my first inclination led me to discount it. But the feeling persisted, forcing my closer examination. I remembered other instances of inspiration and began to recognize a pattern in how the Lord communicates with me. Those patterns of the past teach me how to respond when the Lord presents me with puzzle pieces, and they guide my hand as I work to find the picture in the pieces.

True to lessons learned in high school English and popular culture, I subscribe to the philosophy of carpe diem. We do need to focus on today and live our present as wisely and as richly as possible. At the same time, our past and our future make that possible, strengthening our hand as we strive to seize the moment for all its glory.

Of Lofty Quests and Stubbed Toes
(May 2011)

I have been musing lately about truth. More specifically, I have been musing about the search for truth and the powerful effect that search can have on an individual. I love "light bulb moments," those epiphanies that alter my perspective in significant ways. Those moments have, at times, carried me through dark hours or shaped the course of my thoughts for years. As much as I love epiphanies, however, I recognize that the process leading up to that "aha" lends perhaps more power to my life than the moment itself.

Joseph Smith once said "by proving contraries, truth is made manifest." He spoke in the context of addressing spiritual concerns, although I think the concept applies outside the realm of religion, as well. We occasionally come upon pieces of doctrine (or, perhaps, scientific or sociological evidence) that seem to conflict, either with each other or with our own understanding. As we work through the sometimes long and arduous process of resolving those conflicts, we reach insights about the world around us and, more importantly, about ourselves. Eventually, if we stay with the process to completion, we break out into wonderful vistas of truth. The view is spectacular, but there is no shortcut. Without the climb that preceded it, the mountaintop experience would lack power.

When not grappling with issues of eternal import, I often exercise. (Actually, come to think of it, philosophy and exercise complement each other nicely, but that's a topic for another time.) I set goals for myself to decrease my minutes per mile or increase the weight I push. Anyone dedicated to exercise recognizes the necessity of goals. However, the health benefit does not come when we reach our goal. That 6-minute mile or 400-pound bench press (my husband's goal, not mine) is relatively immaterial, except insofar as it motivates us forward. But the process leading up to that milestone yields incredible health benefits.

I stop short of putting eternal or scientific truth in the same category as an exercise goal. Truth in and of itself ennobles us as individuals and as a society. However, the process of arriving at the truth can prove equally life-changing. A genuine desire for truth, combined with a commitment to stick with the process to its completion, no matter what obstacles arise, builds us brick upon brick.

Eighteen years ago, I found myself unexpectedly in love. I was a young widow, blessed not only with a second chance but also with the assurance (rare, I think) that marrying Brad was the right choice for me. Still, as a lifelong follower of a religion that holds eternal marriage as a central belief, I now faced a dilemma both doctrinal and extremely personal. I had married once in the faith already, a marriage decreed eternal. I now prepared to marry for a second time. I had several options, each with its own degree of pain and each carrying the necessity of faith.

I weighed the options, studied them out. I fasted, prayed, knelt at the gates of heaven and pleaded for understanding. I talked with Brad, with my ecclesiastical leaders. Over a period of months, I gained the understanding I needed. I made my choice and felt peace.

God could have given me the answer at the beginning. Ironically, in fact, He did just that, but having not yet wrestled with the question I was not at that point ready to accept the answer. During the ensuing months of studying and pondering I learned much about eternity, about the blessings

God rains down upon His children, and about my own relationship with my Heavenly Father. Brad and I grew closer together, strengthened through the struggle.

I will always love the "aha" moments, the view from the mountaintop. But I treasure the lessons of the climb, lessons paid for with sweat and aching muscles and toes stubbed from stumbling along in the dark.

Gardens of God

(January 2012)

I spent a morning this week in the LDS temple in St. Louis. For members of the Church of Jesus Christ of Latter-Day Saints, temple worship forms the pinnacle of our religious devotion. Like Solomon's temple in ancient Israel, temples represent our finest workmanship, our most beautiful architecture. While pondering in the temple, I thought of joy and rejoicing, of beauty and God's presence, of gardens, and of the tools of creation.

The Lord intends for us to live with joy and rejoicing. In fact, in 2 Nephi 2:25 (in the *Book of Mormon*) we read that "men are that they might have joy." Through Isaiah, the Lord commands, "But be ye glad and rejoice for ever in that which I create." (Isaiah 65:18)

To the end that we might experience this joy, the Lord created this earth and beautified it. He gave nature not just function but also form and beauty. God left a bit of Himself in the beauty of His creations. Through that beauty, we touch the divine, whether it is in the stretch of moonlight across a quiet lake or through the ethereal song of a wild bird.

Places of beauty figure prominently in the Lord's plan for His children, with gardens forming the backdrop for pivotal events. In the Garden of Eden, Adam and Eve walked and talked with God, enjoying His presence in their innocence. In Eden, He gave them the gift of agency, and they used that agency to set the Lord's plan of salvation in motion.

Transgression made it necessary for Adam and Eve to leave the garden, and forever after humans have experienced the tension between garden and wilderness, between the peace of the Lord's presence and the weeds of everyday life. We learn our greatest lessons in the wilderness of our trials, and we grow stronger as we struggle to reach spaces of beauty and peace. The gardens pull us forward. The wilderness shapes us.

The Savior, Himself, atoned for our sins first in a garden. Though strengthened by His Father's presence there, he bled from every pore as He struggled beneath the weight of the sins and pains of billions of his brothers and sisters. Then the Savior left the Garden of Gethsemane, only to suffer all that pain a second time in the foul air of Golgotha, for a time utterly alone. It was critical to the plan that He accomplish this part of the atonement outside of God's presence.

Finally, as the early morning sun stretched over yet another garden, Jesus rose from the dead, bringing hope to a world languishing in darkness. A lovely stained glass window at the Carmel of the Holy Trinity in Spokane, Washington depicts the scene outside the garden tomb. In fact, we owe much of our understanding of religion to the artists and composers who have brought the scriptures to life through the centuries.

Medieval theologians believed that light, as the first act of God's creation, represented the purest manifestation of divine presence. For hundreds of years, artisans have carefully crafted stained glass windows designed to bring that divine light into the worship services of churches throughout the world. Other artists bring beauty through music, dance, poetry and sculpture. Ordinary people live lives of beauty that inspire those around them.

When we create, particularly when we create beauty, we access the spark of God within us. We draw on inspiration and form a partnership with the Creator. At the same time, on those occasions when our creations approach true beauty, they provide a vehicle for the audience to step into the presence of God, if only for an instant.

Years ago, I sat in a dark theater on New Year's Eve, enjoying Burlington, Vermont's First Night celebration and ready to applaud any event that kept me out of the frigid New England air for a few minutes. The curtain opened, and I sat back in my chair, stunned. A group of dancers, some disabled and some not, kept me entranced for the next half an hour with one of the most profoundly moving dance performances I have ever experienced. Lines between traditional dancer and disabled dancer blurred. Fear and pain and stigma melted away, leaving just the aching beauty of the dance. No sellout performance of the New York City Ballet could have touched my soul more deeply.

I ponder my own opportunity to create moments of beauty for those around me. I no longer dance, and I never claimed any ability to bring canvas or stained glass to life. All the same, I can find my own tools, my own way to live a life of beauty. St. Francis of Assisi said simply, "God is beauty." I look to reach toward God, to build gardens in my life.

Loving Away the Fear

(June 2012)

My children have died a hundred deaths in my imagination, and my heart has broken over and over again. My bank account has run dry; my house has burnt to the ground; my car has careened off cliffs and into trees; intruders invade my home on dark nights. Is it peculiar to women, this almost irresistible tendency to pre-live the possibility of tragedy and lie awake in midnight fear?

I remind myself that worry accomplishes nothing good. Fretting does nothing to prepare me for the actual tragedies of life, big or little, nor does my imagining a scenario provide some sort of mystical immunization against real danger. Quite the opposite, in fact. Worry interrupts my sleep, shifts my focus from matters of greater importance, and wastes hours I could more productively donate to joy.

Recently, as I pondered the relationship between worry and fear and our inability to feel love and fear at the same time, I began to chew on the possibility that incorporating greater love into my life could provide an antidote to the worry that gnaws away at my equilibrium. My ponderings led me to the scripture in 1 John 4:18 that reads:

> *"There is no fear in love; but perfect love casteth out fear: because fear hath torment. He that feareth is not made perfect in love."*

I sensed a key in that verse somewhere and began to study it in context. I discovered a rich lesson on love in 1 John 4. That "perfect love," the love that casts out fear, is the love of Christ. It is not my power or my love that casts out Satan and the fear and worry that he inspires, as if I could love myself up that tower of Babel to reach godly power. Rather, it is the love and power of the Savior Himself. Negativity and fear flee in the face of His spirit and His grace.

My part, then, is to accept into my life the spirit and grace that the Savior offers. I bring that spirit into my life by loving others, by knowing and emulating Jesus Christ, and by trusting God. Believing that He loves me, trusting in that love, gives me the key to casting out fear. That ability to trust, to truly live a Christlike life, takes time and experience, repentance and work. Unfortunately for impatient souls like me, there is no shortcut. I come to know God bit by bit through the years as I study and as I hike the peaks and valleys of life. Fortunately, God possesses an extraordinary abundance of patience and a willingness to shower blessings and peace upon me just as quickly as I can open my heart enough to hold them.

Ultimately, having the Holy Spirit dwell in me and feeling that trust are gifts of God that I need to prepare to receive. The more I give place for the perfect love of the Savior in my soul, the more fear and worry fade away. As I cease to fear, I can eventually feel the peace of being "made perfect in love." Then what will I do with those midnight hours? And how will the world spin on its way without my worry to hold it aloft?

This I Believe

(September 2012)

I should state up front that I believe in God. Moreover, I'm a Christian. And I try to be a pretty obedient Christian. With a lot of commandments available for keeping or breaking, sometimes a person can get a little overwhelmed. When I need a dose of simplicity, I look to the first commandments from God and the ones He said He thought were the most important. I think of God telling Adam and Eve in the garden to raise children and take good care of the earth. It probably sounded easy then, with flowers all around and no crying children or rebellious teenagers. Later on, in the confusion of opinions in Jerusalem, the Savior's commandments to love God and love other people may have given folks a little more pause to reflect. Still, I think those few guiding principles can lead to a good life, and I try to follow them with more or less success from day to day. Do things that would please God. Love other people, without regard for their color or nationality, their economic status or philosophical preference, the style of their clothes or their ability to conform to social norms. Treat the environment with respect. Raise my children to seek beyond themselves and make the world a better place.

For me, beauty plays an essential role in that process. I seek for beauty in nature, in art, in people, in life experience. I believe I have both the ability and the responsibility to create, discover and share beauty in its many forms.

One hundred years ago, Raymond Macdonald Alden (most famously known for his story "Why the Chimes Rang") wrote a story about a marvelous palace built by the combined music of an accidental orchestra of musicians. I believe in music and its power to create palaces in our souls and bridge the gaps that separate us from others. That music can take many forms and still reach the soul in vital ways—from professional chamber music, to the aching notes of soul or country, to an amateur musician with just the right inspiration or just the right occasion. I hear music in the melody of a life well lived and in the jubilation of a challenge met and conquered. I love the story of the palace built by music, and I love that the musicians had to combine their notes together for the creation to commence. It feels so true and so possible.

I believe that we cannot live life fully as hermits, that human relationships are an integral part of our development and the richness of our lives. I believe that serving others leads us to the discovery of ourselves and is essential if we want to explore the boundaries of our potential as individuals and as a society.

I believe that each of us is, at the core, essentially spiritual, and that our spiritual core at some point begins to yearn for its source of light. If we ignore that need, we risk destabilizing ourselves. The quest for the source of light and for an understanding of our relationship to that light can define our life in wonderful ways, even though at times the journey can prove unsettling. As a parent, I believe I have the responsibility to give my children the tools they need for their own spiritual quest: an understanding of the language of the spirit, a desire to seek, and a solid base from which to start. We need to believe. It gives us root.

No Apologies; I Am a Believer

(September 2013—This piece appeared originally on the Mormon Women blog.)

Who am I? I am a writer, or at least I aspire to be one. I am a teacher. I am a wife and mother. And I am a believer.

Why am I Mormon? I came by my religion the easy way. I inherited it from folks like my Great-Great Grandmother Decker who crossed the plains as an almost single mother and helped found Parowan, Utah. But my faith, the reason I stay? Now that raises a different question entirely. My wilderness hikes and forest prayers have never led me to burning bushes or shining pillars of light. No angel ever stopped my tracks on the road to Damascus.

And yet, like the Savior's companions in a storm-tossed boat, I have received the witness of peace. I have read the scriptures, seeking for wisdom, and marveled as words once spoken to prophets took new life in direct answer to my pleading. I have knelt in prayer and felt the warmth of the Comforter envelop me. I have taken the advice of the *Book of Mormon* prophet Alma to "experiment upon the word" (Alma 32:27), acting on subtle promptings, and I have watched my faith grow as the Lord took my hand.

I have a dear friend who challenges my faith. She cannot fathom how I can accept the history of polygamy in The Church of Jesus Christ of Latter-Day Saints or support a priesthood to which I cannot be ordained. I have thought a great deal about that. Every Mormon woman at some point has to grapple with her relationship to these issues of faith and others like them, and unfortunately epiphanies come with a built-in "non-transferrable" clause. God knows the value of a good test of faith, and pioneer ancestry hardly makes one immune to the need for conversion.

For me, that conversion has come in stages. As a young adult, fresh out of the comfortable arms of home, I read scriptures on a mountainside in Wyoming and recognized a tender mercy in the magnificent double rainbow that appeared just when I needed a creative "hello" from my Heavenly Father. As a young widow, I came to the quiet realization that God's plan of happiness was true. The plan became more than merely a lesson taught by young missionaries or enthusiastic Sunday School teachers. We really do live again. Families can last forever.

And here, in my middle age, I am beginning to learn to trust in God's love for me, for all of His children. I have seen too many prayers answered to claim coincidence. Joseph Smith once said, "I had seen a vision; I knew it, and I knew that God knew it, and I could not deny it, neither dared I do it; at least I knew that by so doing I would offend God, and come under condemnation." (Joseph Smith-History 1:25)

While the angel Moroni very kindly lets me sleep at night, God has sent me numerous angels from all walks of life. He continues to supply the wisdom that I lack. I cannot deny that. I am a believer.

Not Just Good, but True

(May 2014)

I belong to a church that claims to be the true church of Jesus Christ, restored by God Himself in modern times. This is a bold claim, to be sure, a sometimes unpopular claim in Christian circles. In a religious environment where the trend favors an "all paths lead to God" philosophy, the notion of a single path seems exclusive, restrictive.

Recently, I broke my usual rule of avoiding blogs that blast the Church of Jesus Christ of Latter-Day Saints (LDS). I find such blogs and the accompanying comments divisive, contentious and frankly painful to read. However, someone I respect posted a link to a blog, and I took the bait. At the end of the essay, I found a comment that has caused me to ponder. Presumably defending the LDS (or Mormon) faith, the commenter wrote the following:

"I think a very large problem people have is judging a religion by trying to determine if it is "true." It's just not what religion is about. Good inclusive and loving religion is about goodness, not about truth. It's easy to disprove any religion technically - or any other superstition. Rejecting Mormonism by finding it untrue is silly. Judge it for its goodness. No religion is "true." Religions vary a great deal in how good they are, and Mormonism is one of the very best."

Religion is not about truth? Really? If religion is not about truth, then what, exactly, is the purpose of religion? I can join a club or a social movement if I need an organization to help me to do good, effect positive change in the world. But I want something more powerful than that. I want the power that comes with having faith in something absolutely unshakeable, something greater than the universe, something beyond human control. I want truth.

I realize, in my quest for truth, that I will have to sacrifice to obtain it. I may have to sacrifice the comfort of personal habit or public opinion. I expect to work and find myself pushed to my limits occasionally, because I have never had a truly amazing moment of clarity and beauty that came without sweat or tears. In fact, the LDS prophet Joseph Smith once taught that "a religion that does not require the sacrifice of all things never has the power sufficient to produce the faith necessary unto life and salvation."

While Joseph Smith may not resonate with everyone, the concept that the worthwhile things of life require sacrifice certainly seems to resonate with people of all cultures and persuasions. Interestingly, as our modern culture moves away from organized religion, we seem to create our own sacrifices to replace those formerly imposed by the religions we shun. Record numbers of athletes run marathons and ultra marathons each year. Fitness enthusiasts from teenagers to grandmothers groan under the strain of a daily crossfit workout. We eat bitter kale and forego gluten and sugar and meat (which makes the *Whole Foods* skit by Studio C particularly hilarious). We sacrifice our families and our joy to devote most of our waking hours to our careers. We search and search and search…for truth, though we may phrase it differently.

So I will be bold and declare my search for absolute truth. I believe I have found the avenue (or perhaps the container) for that truth in the Church of Jesus Christ of Latter-Day Saints, not because the LDS church sets itself apart and closes its doors against the tenets of other faiths or the discoveries of science or academia, but precisely because the gospel encompasses and accepts all truth. The grandfather of LDS apostle Henry B. Eyring once told his son, "…in this church you don't have to believe anything that isn't true. You go over to the University of Arizona and learn everything you can, and whatever is true is part of the gospel." I have always loved that quote and have let it inform my life.

Another concept that I find critical in my search for truth and God is the notion that truth comes to me when I act, whether that action involves serving others, enduring with grace or wrestling through to the solution of a spiritual conundrum. Eugene England, an LDS intellectual, once wrote an essay called "Why the Church is as True as the Gospel," an essay that has proved pivotal for me in how I approach my religious life.

In the essay, Mr. England points out that "the (LDS) Church is as 'true,' as effective, as sure an instrument of salvation as the system of doctrines we call the gospel-and that that is so in good part because of the very flaws, human exasperations, and historical problems that occasionally give us all some anguish." We all experience the frustrations of imperfect leaders, doctrines that may clash with our comfortable existence or with each other, or opportunities to serve with those who may drive us to the point of insanity with their habits or prejudices. But as we seek divine guidance in working through these exasperations, and as we act rather than grumble (or even act while grumbling, sometimes), we eventually push through to astonishing vistas of truth that we could not have understood without the struggle. We come to know Jesus Christ by walking in His footsteps for a time.

Yes, religion should be loving and inclusive, should inspire goodness in the community it serves. And if a religion is to truly save souls and offer the riches of eternity, it should also be true.

When the Cup Does Not Pass

(January 2015)

Like many LDS children, I began each school year armed with a priesthood blessing of counsel and comfort from my father. Invariably, that blessing promised me "learning experiences" during the course of the year. I soon realized that those experiences generally came accompanied by an uncomfortable amount of pain and frustration.

True to Dad's inspiration, I have had many opportunities over the years to learn through trials. Those difficult periods have taught me bits of empathy and a degree of humility. Scriptures have come alive as they suddenly felt more applicable than ever before. I understand more about unconditional love now, about the blessings of suffering, the purifying role of sacrifice, the freedom of forgiving and seeking forgiveness. I rarely seek for learning experiences, but I do appreciate them (sometimes through gritted teeth). I appreciate that the process of feeling stretched to the point of breaking makes me stronger and allows me to see the hand of God and the compassion of others in my life. I love the epiphany moments, even if they come in the pit. After all, a light shines brighter in a dark cellar than in the light of noonday.

But what about those times when we hit bottom and keep going, or when we hit bottom repeatedly without the hoped for relief, without the brilliant light of understanding? Christians of all faiths (my own included) love to quote 1 Corinthians 10:13 and point out that God will not give us more than we can handle. I agree that God is faithful, that He will provide a way to escape temptation. I have less confidence saying that God will never allow us to be submitted to a trial beyond our own capacity to "handle it."

Purging Experiences

And so we arrive at what I see as the difference between learning experiences and purging experiences, experiences that help us to become new creatures. Sometimes, the bottom keeps dropping. Sometimes, the relief and the insight fail to come. Sometimes, we cannot handle the pain or find the answers. The trial continues unrelenting, and we feel our spirits crush under the pressure. We stand before God, naked and head bowed, and say, "I can go no further. This is all I have to offer." And He gently hands us the bitter cup. It feels cruel, like a cosmic joke at our expense. We may feel abandoned. But I think if only we could see the love in God's eyes as He extends the cup, we might begin to change our perspective.

Long ago, Elder James E. Faust gave a talk about the refiner's fire. In the talk, he used the example of the Martin handcart company, an ill-fated company of Mormon pioneers that ran into harsh conditions crossing the plains. Fully one quarter of the members of the company perished on the way West. All endured great suffering. And yet, not one of that company abandoned the faith. As one survivor said years later:

> *"Everyone of us came through with the absolute knowledge that God lives for we became acquainted with him in our extremities. ...*

> *"'Was I sorry that I chose to come by handcart? No. Neither then nor any minute of my life since. The price we paid to become acquainted with God was a privilege to pay.'"*

Elder Faust explained: "Here then is a great truth. In the pain, the agony, and the heroic endeavors of life, we pass through a refiner's fire, and the insignificant and the unimportant in our lives can melt away like dross and make our faith bright, intact, and strong. In this way the divine image can be mirrored from the soul. It is part of the purging toll exacted of some to become acquainted with God. In the agonies of life, we seem to listen better to the faint, godly whisperings of the Divine Shepherd."

President Harold B. Lee said something similar: "There is a refining process that comes through suffering, I think, that we can't experience any other way than by suffering. ... We draw closer to Him who gave His life that man might be. We feel a kinship that we have never felt before. ... He suffered more than we can ever imagine. But to the extent that we have suffered, somehow it seems to have the effect of drawing us closer to the divine, helps to purify our souls, and helps to purge out the things that are not pleasing in the sight of the Lord. ... We must be refined. We must be tested in order to prove the strength and power that are in us."

Purging Helps Us to Transform

I have noticed lately that these purging experiences seem to occur most often in conjunction with a commitment to a new phase of discipleship. One friend recommitted to her faith after several years apart and almost immediately experienced debilitating health problems. Another finally relinquished an addiction of decades and found unexpected trials that rocked his confidence. Positive transformation does not always immediately result in blessings. Occasionally, a purging accompanies such a transformation. I believe there are at least two reasons for this.

First, as we become new people, we must necessarily shed our former lives, slough off the trappings of the people we used to be. As Elder Faust suggested above, the refiner's fire melts away the dross, and we experience a rebirth.

Second, at times we doubt our own transformation. Have we truly repented? Are we strong enough to hold to this new commitment we have made? Will our conversion stick? Abraham made a covenant with the Lord that would shape the world for generations to come. God promised that he would be a father of many nations. And then God asked Abraham to sacrifice the miracle son, the very posterity He had promised. Elder Hugh B. Brown said of that sacrifice that God knew perfectly well that Abraham would sacrifice anything He asked, but that "Abraham needed to learn something about Abraham." Likewise, when we come through these purging experiences, having made the sacrifice asked of us, we, like Abraham, can know that our transformation is real, that we are truly committed to God. We need that confidence that comes with knowing ourselves.

Is There No Other Way?

My husband posed an intriguing question as we discussed these purging experiences recently. "Is there no positive way to become a new person? Why does this refining process always have to be painful and negative?" I pondered that question for some time. The refining process seems to work best through pain that brings us literally and figuratively to our knees, that forces us to acknowledge our nothingness before the Lord. I thought about why that is, about what the refiner's fire accomplishes in us. The process seems to accomplish several key purposes:

- We come to recognize our complete dependence on God. We feel a great need.

- We accept God's will unconditionally.

- We relinquish everything that gets between us and God: every sin, every wish, every bit of our own agenda.

- The Spirit burns within us. (This is where the true purging occurs.)

- We see things from an eternal perspective.

- We are willing to sacrifice whatever God asks of us.

- Our prayers become true communication.

President Spencer W. Kimball spoke of the process of revelation, and as I listened to his words, I was struck with how closely that experience of a prophet desiring revelation resembled the experience of a person going through transformation. The counsel President Kimball gave in the context of seeking critical revelation seems to apply here. He said:

"Do you want guidance? Have you prayed to the Lord for inspiration? Do you want to do right or do you want to do what you want to do whether or not it is right? Do you want to do what is best for you in the long run or what seems more desirable for the moment? Have you prayed? How much have you prayed? How did you pray? Have you prayed as did the Savior of the world in Gethsemane or did you ask for what you want regardless of its being proper? Do you say in your prayers: 'Thy will be done'? Did you say, 'Heavenly Father, if you will inspire and impress me with the right, I will do that right'? Or, did you pray, 'Give me what I want or I will take it anyway'? Did you say: 'Father in Heaven, I love you, I believe in you, I know you are omniscient. I am honest. I am sincerely desirous of doing right. I know you can see the end from the beginning. You can see the future. You can discern if under this situation I present, I will have peace or turmoil, happiness or sorrow, success or failure. Tell me, please, loved Heavenly Father, and I promise to do what you

tell me to do.' Have you prayed that way? Don't you think it might be wise? Are you courageous enough to pray that prayer?"

In short, are we courageous enough to truly stand naked before God and acknowledge that we are nothing without Him? Can we give it all up in order to become what God has designed for us to become?

Thorns That Heal

The ancient Apostle Paul spoke of a thorn in the flesh (2 Corinthians 12:7-10) that he had begged the Lord to remove. "For this thing I besought the Lord thrice, that it might depart from me," he said. God did not remove the thorn. Whether that thorn represented a physical malady, an addiction from which Paul craved to be healed, an enemy who refused to back down, or some other trial, we do not know. But we do know that Paul eventually accepted the thorn as a part of his mortal experience, as a gift from God to help him to be strong.

If we accept it, God will offer deliverance through our refiner's fire. We may not find the trial removed. In fact, the fire itself may become our deliverance if we can develop the ability to trust God enough to hand our trials over to Him.

James E. Faust said, "Out of the refiner's fire can come a glorious deliverance. It can be a noble and lasting rebirth. The price to become acquainted with God will have been paid. There can come a sacred peace. There will be a reawakening of dormant, inner resources. A comfortable cloak of righteousness will be drawn around us to protect us and to keep us warm spiritually. Self-pity will vanish as our blessings are counted."

Sources

- April 1979 General Conference, Elder James E. Faust, "The Refiner's Fire"

- *Teachings of Presidents of the Church: Harold B. Lee*, Chapter 21: "Striving for Perfection"

- "Power from Abrahamic Tests," by Truman G. Madsen, Meridian Magazine, http://www.ldsmag.com

- *Teachings of Presidents of the Church: Spencer W. Kimball*, Chapter 22: Revelation: "A Continuous Melody and a Thunderous Appeal"

Building a Healthy Soul

(March 2015—text of a talk given in church)

Join me on a walk in a lovely garden, the Garden of Eden to be precise. You remember the story: God creates a beautiful garden and places Adam in the garden. He gives Adam a commandment. Genesis 2:15-17 describes that commandment:

> *15 And the Lord God took the man, and put him into the Garden of Eden to dress it and to keep it.*
>
> *16 And the Lord God commanded the man, saying, Of every tree of the garden thou mayest freely eat:*
>
> *17 But of the tree of the knowledge of good and evil, thou shalt not eat of it: for in the day that thou eatest thereof thou shalt surely die.*

Commandment given, God creates Eve, and the first couple go merrily on their way, enjoying their innocence and the beauties around them. Satan tempts Eve, who eats of the forbidden fruit and shares the fruit with Adam. And thus the plan of salvation is born. Adam and Eve become mortal, subject to both physical and spiritual death. They know good from evil and can now experience both sorrow and joy. For the first time, they have agency, because they have both opposition and knowledge. They bear children, and God provides a Savior so that Adam and Eve and their posterity can have the opportunity to once again live with God.

I find it interesting that God uses a commandment that is essentially physical (a commandment about what to eat) to introduce His plan of salvation for the entire universe. Not only is the first commandment a physical commandment, but the consequences involve a mix of the physical and spiritual. I have thought about this a great deal. We tend to consider the spiritual as more Godlike than the physical, as if our bodies hold us back and limit us in some way, but I doubt that the Lord sees it that way at all.

One of my favorite scriptures illuminates for me how God feels about the relationship of our physical bodies and our spirits. In Doctrine & Covenants 88:15, we read "And the spirit and the body are the soul of man." To me, that means that our eternal soul requires both the spirit and the body, that both components are critical. Additional scriptures bear that out. Daniel refuses to eat the king's rich food, and he is blessed with great wisdom. The Savior fasts for a long period to prepare Himself to begin His ministry, and so forth.

Back to Adam and Eve. Do you remember the consequences of eating the forbidden fruit? Adam and Eve became mortal, of course, and they had to leave the Garden of Eden. In Genesis 3:17, God says something curious to Adam. "Cursed is the ground for thy sake." For thy sake! As if the thorns and weeds were a blessing! But they were, just as Eve's pain and sorrow in childbearing were a blessing. Somehow, those physical challenges were critical for Adam and Eve and for us in our quest to become like God. They help us to grow and learn, and they help us to understand God and what it means to be godlike.

Think about it from an exercise perspective. Unless I literally rip my muscles, I will not grow stronger. And in order to build that muscle, I have to push against something. I have to have opposition. God created the physical and spiritual experiences to run in tandem.

How Does That Apply to Me?

My patriarchal blessing includes a phrase that I return to again and again. In my blessing, God counsels me that as I keep my body in good condition, I will be more responsive to the promptings of the Spirit. That promise is not unique to me. Think of the Word of Wisdom, our famous code of health. We are commanded regarding what to eat and what not to eat, and then God spells out the promises. We will receive health, we will run and not be weary…and in verse 19, we learn that we will "find wisdom and great treasures of knowledge, even hidden treasures." I think God cares a great deal about what we do with our bodies, as well as with our spirits. He even refers to our bodies as temples, and if you have ever had the chance to visit one of our LDS temples, you know how beautiful they are and what care is taken to keep them beautiful and pure.

In his October 2014 General Conference talk, Elder Jörg Klebingat outlines six tools to help us reach the point where we can approach the throne of God with confidence. I find it instructive that the first two suggestions he gives us are rather bold directives to take responsibility for our own spiritual well-being and to take responsibility for our own physical well-being. "Stop justifying and stop making excuses," he says, reminding us that Heavenly Father knows each of our circumstances perfectly.

Elder Klebingat continues, "Feeding the spirit while neglecting the body, which is a temple, usually leads to spiritual dissonance and lowered self-esteem." I think we can safely say that the reverse is true, as well. If we focus on our physical health and neglect our spirits, we will also suffer. But if we feed and exercise both body and spirit, then our potential is great.

What Have I Learned?

I have learned that I can endure and that if I push myself, I can grow stronger. I have started to run more over the last couple of years. I am not a great runner, but I find that I quite enjoy it. Sometimes, though, it is difficult to take those first steps or to keep going after a few tough miles on not quite enough sleep. When the wind chill is -15, I struggle to put on my shoes and open my front door. But I can tell you that the exhilaration I feel after running a 10K in that kind of cold is amazing! I feel like superwoman. So then, when faced with something in life that pushes me to my limits, I tell myself, "If I can run 6 miles in sub zero weather, I can absolutely meet this challenge I am facing now."

I have learned that opposition is necessary. I want nicely sculpted arms, and I want to be strong enough so that I do not need to call my husband every time I need to move something heavy. But I will never build that muscle definition unless I push heavy weight. The same thing is true in my spiritual life. Brad and I have been through some years in our marriage that took us near to the breaking point. We dealt with some heavy opposition, and because of that, we grew closer together. We learned a great deal about God and about faith. I have had experiences that brought me to my knees again and again, and I would not trade them for anything. The apostle Paul learned a similar lesson. In 2 Corinthians 12:7-10, he tells about a thorn in the flesh that he had to endure and what he learned from that:

7 And lest I should be exalted above measure through the abundance of the revelations, there was given to me a thorn in the flesh, the messenger of Satan to buffet me, lest I should be exalted above measure.

8 For this thing I besought the Lord thrice, that it might depart from me.

9 And he said unto me, My grace is sufficient for thee: for my strength is made perfect in weakness. Most gladly therefore will I rather glory in my infirmities, that the power of Christ may rest upon me.

10 Therefore I take pleasure in infirmities, in reproaches, in necessities, in persecutions, in distresses for Christ's sake: for when I am weak, then am I strong.

I have learned that I need to exercise every day. Intense, but sporadic, exercise does little to increase my strength or endurance. By the same token, we need to read scriptures every day, pray every day, go to church every week, and so forth. Elder Klebingat says that we need to "apply the atonement of Christ daily."

I have learned that I have to take care of myself with nutrition and rest. The scriptures remind us not to run faster than we have strength. In both physical and spiritual pursuits, we need to pace ourselves. A couple of years ago, I made the astonishing discovery that I like to run, so I fairly quickly built up to five mile runs. Predictably, I developed tendonitis, and I had to pull way back for a time. I learned that I need to build up my mileage slowly and let my body adjust. By the same token, if we try to live all of the commandments perfectly all at once, go to the temple three times a week, make fresh bread for everyone in the ward and read scriptures for hours each day, we will quickly burn out.

I have learned that I have to obey certain laws to get certain results. If I eat more calories than I burn, I will gain fat. If I eat too much sugar, I will feel sluggish. On the other hand, if I eat healthy foods and get adequate rest, I will have energy and think more clearly. Likewise, in D&C 130: 20-21, we learn that when we obtain any blessing from God, it is by obedience to that law upon which it is predicated.

But, Wow, It's Hard!

The reality is, we are going to fall a lot. We're going to fall out of the habit of reading scriptures, or we are going to eat an entire pint of Ben & Jerry's ice cream in one sitting. We are going to deal with addictions or struggle with our callings. We are going to have crises of faith and physical ailments that stop us in our tracks. Heavenly Father knows that. Elder D. Todd Christofferson said the following in the October 2014 General Conference:

> *"I am under no illusion that this can be achieved by our own efforts alone without [the Savior's] very substantial and constant help. 'We know that it is by grace that we are saved, after all we can do.' And we do not need to achieve some minimum level of capacity or goodness before God will help—divine aid can be ours every hour of every day, no matter where we are in the path of obedience. But I know that beyond desiring His help, we must exert ourselves, repent, and choose God for Him to be able to act in our lives consistent with justice and moral agency. My plea is simply to take responsibility and go to work so that there is something for God to help us with."*

That is our challenge, to go to work so that God has something to work with. Take the next step. That may involve reading a verse of scripture a day or walking around the block, or it may involve getting the help you need to overcome an addiction. Do something, take a step down the road to a healthy soul.

Inspired by Art and Literature

Mountains and Valleys

(January 2011)

"I have descended from a planet called grief," says the Count of Monte Cristo, explaining the source of his almost superhuman wisdom. "He who has felt the deepest grief is best able to experience supreme happiness. We must have felt what it is to die. . . that we may appreciate the enjoyment of living."

While some view the Count as almost godlike, this man who dares to manipulate fate falls into the oh so human error of prescribing his own medicine to others. The grief that Edmond Dantes suffered for 14 years in prison, the grief that took away everything dear to him and brought him to the point of suicide, finally ennobled him until he emerged as the supernally wise and unfathomably wealthy Count of Monte Cristo. He plays God--or perhaps the antithesis thereof--arranging the lives of those he hates and those he loves so that they, too, can experience the destructive or ennobling power of grief.

While I cannot bring myself to complete agreement with the Count's philosophy and the liberties he takes in applying it in the lives of others, I do recognize the power of pain in my own life. Just as I relish the energizing feeling of completing a taxing workout, I love the empowerment of having passed through adversity. When I finish a good run, the blood pumps through my veins. My skin tingles, I breathe more deeply, and even my mind feels cleansed and sharpened. Similarly, looking back on a time of trial I sense a new strength, unforeseen insights, more faith in the possibilities of the future. I feel alive.

In college, after a year of grappling with the frustrating fallout of silly teenage highs and lows, I decided to teach myself to shut off those annoying emotional reactions. Who really needs to ache over boys, anyway? I succeeded frighteningly well, and for a few months I enjoyed a respite from tears and heart hiccups. After a time, however, I began to miss the chance to cry my soul clean. I needed a searing ache to wipe away the sludge of leftover worries and nagging doubts. In locking tight the fear and the sorrow, I had also stifled the belly laughs and the astonishing awe of simple bliss. I craved the heights and depths and longed to explore my own boundaries again.

Over time, life reminded me how to double over in pain and gasp in delight. At first I borrowed from the experiences of others: imagining the depths of a mother's sorrow in losing her son to cancer or marveling at a friend's willingness to give herself over to the joyful awkwardness of falling in love. I even determined, with some reluctance, that God gave women hormones for the very purpose of regularly reminding us how to feel.

I love the ability to abandon myself to laughter or tears, knowing from experience that I will eventually regain even ground. I love the cleansing and strengthening power that comes from enduring the depths and pushing the heavy weight. I cherish the gift of empathy that comes only with experience. I cannot say that I crave pain or ask for trials, but I fear them a little less now than I used to. In the words of our dear Count of Monte Cristo, "All human wisdom is summed up in these two words, 'Wait and hope.'"

Enchanted Always

(January 2011)

I have discovered a new hero in Lotty Wilkins, thanks to my book group and their decision to choose a cozy, feel good book for the dead of winter. Lotty blossoms on the pages of Elizabeth von Armin's *The Enchanted April*, the story of four women who share a small Italian castle for a month.

We stumble upon the nearly invisible Mrs. Wilkins in her club on a dreary afternoon, little suspecting how the wisteria and the Mediterranean sunshine will transform her, giving her substance and glow.

Just the hint of wisteria in a newspaper ad is enough to begin the metamorphosis, and our Mrs. Wilkins gathers an unlikely combination of roommates for her impulsive vacation: Mrs. Arbuthnot, the efficient and sad church lady with a penchant for classifying the poor; Mrs. Fisher, a woman of respectability, memories and her own importance; and Lady Caroline, the beautiful and rather selfish blue blood of the group. Ah, you see how easy it is to slide each woman quickly into her proper envelope!

Yet somehow Lotty fails to see the obvious envelopes, first because her sense of her own awkwardness blinds her and then because the flowers of San Salvatore impose their beauty on everything she sees. Lotty expects heaven and therefore finds her paradise in the gardens and people around her. Though she does not realize it, that, more than the sunshine and wisteria, makes up the infectious magic of San Salvatore.

I think perhaps Lotty's expectation of beauty and her willingness to allow those around her to transform against the odds are the qualities that have set me pondering this week. Whether it's Lotty's faith in individuals, the magic of San Salvatore, or simply a delicious and unexpected reality of life, the characters in the novel do melt and soften and blossom, bursting out of the cubbyholes fashioned for them by the reader and by the characters themselves.

I find the scent of lilies and roses wafting into my own wintry week, and I begin to wonder if the expectation of beauty can hold the same power outside of fiction, away from garden paths and the flowering Judas tree. One could rightly call Lotty naïve and warn of the dangers of blindly expecting goodness, but sometimes I find that a little naïveté and a spritz of danger enhance loveliness. More often than not, we find what we expect to find in life, in our spouses, in the day that waits just outside our bedroom door.

Looking ahead to the next few weeks of winter, I propose to jump straight into lilies and expectations of sunshine. Why not? April and San Salvatore have plenty of enchantment to share with a prairie winter and soul ready to be delighted.

Falling in Love

(April 2011)

I have fallen in love once again, this time compliments of my, um, electronic book reader. I refrain from naming the brand, since I have not fallen in love with any particular features of the device but rather with the library I now carry in my purse. My psyche craves prose, and I have periodically neglected to feed the addiction, a sin of omission that always manages to set me just a bit off kilter and leave me yearning.

In the months since Christmas I have wandered the tunnels underneath Washington D.C. with Dan Brown in *The Lost Symbol* (a disappointment, I must confess) and followed the Count of Monte Cristo along his path of revenge and redemption (much more satisfying). I found Elizabeth Von Arnin's *The Enchanted April* simply delicious and Ruth Riechl's autobiography (*Tender at the Bone*) surprisingly intriguing. David Baldacci kept me turning pages, as he always does, and I sauntered through an unusual juxtaposition of Mark Twain's social commentary and Elizabeth Gilbert's introspective *Eat, Pray, Love*.

Then, in a nod to the literary studies of my college days, I opened F. Scott Fitzgerald's *This Side of Paradise*. The other authors gave me much to entertain and even to ponder, but I feast on Fitzgerald as if savoring my first truly satisfying meal after days of snacking on crackers and cheese. I read with a journal at my side and find myself forming essays in my head comparing the sentimental to the romantic or analyzing the development of Amory's character through the mirror of his relationships.

I promise to spare you the bulk of the literary analysis. Suffice it to say that, for me, literature fills an essential block in the food pyramid. "I have to have a soul," says Fitzgerald's Amory. "I can't be rational--and I won't be molecular." While I have my rational moments, now and again, I also have to have a soul. And that soul needs a steady diet of literature, nature, the full spectrum of emotions, a healthy dose of the spiritual, and moments of peace to write and reflect and pull it all together.

Frederick Moments

(August 2011)

Sunday afternoons at our house are sacred. After lazy naps for the older folks and an hour or two of reading and dolls for the younger folks, we gather in the living room for family time. For us, family time usually involves cards of some sort and a giant bowl of popcorn that empties all too quickly.

This weekend, while someone with a better hand than mine sorted through cards and determined strategy, I looked around at my family. My daughter, too young to effectively manage the strategy of bidding, chatted away happily with Grandma on the phone, recounting her first days of kindergarten. Coach Dad and the 11-year old discussed the previous day's surprise win over a rival football team and replayed my son's two fumble recoveries. Our lone teenager laughed at someone's silly joke, and we all joined in, unable to resist his contagious cheeriness. Hundreds of miles away in Texas, our missionary son enjoyed his first Sunday in the field. Mission experiences are the "coolest thing ever" he wrote in his weekly email. It was a Frederick moment, everyone happy and trouble far away.

I still have a copy of my favorite book from childhood. Leo Leonni tells the story of a chatty family of field mice preparing for winter. Four of the mice busily gather corn and nuts, while Frederick sits off by himself. When they chide him for not working, the quiet mouse says, "I do work. I gather sun rays...and colors...and words, for the winter days are long and many."

When the first snow begins to fall, the mice retreat cheerily to their home in the old stone wall. They eat corn and tell stories. But then the food begins to run out, and the cold drags on. "What about your supplies, Frederick?" they ask. Frederick speaks of the sun, and the mice begin to feel warmer. He speaks of colors, and they see them "as clearly as if they had been painted in their minds." Summer has found them.

Like any mother, I lie awake some nights, frozen at the thought of the horrible things that could happen to my children: kidnappings à la Elizabeth Smart, random accidents, a young child lost in the crowd, or the painful consequences of bad choices. Night terrors respond sluggishly to logic. But in the sanity of daylight I remind myself of Frederick and the power his supplies hold for my children.

Every golden hour of family laughter, each hug, the quiet moments when inspiration washes over the seeking mind, the tears of gratitude, story time with Dad and gloriously untidy choruses of "Sweet Violets"...all add up in the storage room of the heart. In times of emotional famine or the bitter winter of adversity, when I cannot reach out to hold my children in my arms, I have to trust that they can bring forth those colors and bask in the warmth of remembered joy and the surety of love.

Olympics of the Heart

(August 2012)

I had an Olympic moment this morning--a throwback to the 2010 Olympics, actually. Alec's CD blared kd lang when I turned on the truck this morning, and it took me back to the opening ceremonies of the Vancouver Olympics, to a moment that for some reason struck me to the core. Even if kd lang leaves you a little flat, stay with me. This post is really much more about love than music. I wrote this two years ago, but the feelings still hit me every time I hear "Hallelujah."

I love the Olympics, from the record-breaking runs to the heart-breaking spills. For the Vancouver 2010 Olympics, however, the defining moment for me came in the opening ceremonies, when kd lang sang the anthem "Hallelujah." I sat still, electrified, from the opening notes of the song. I do not really know what it was, precisely, that held me mesmerized. As Alec says, "She's got some pipes." But it was not just the amazing voice. The magical marriage of kd lang's voice with Leonard Cohen's poetry produced something greater than either of them.

Alec downloaded the song to his iPod recently, and more often than not he plays it during our pre-dawn drive to seminary. At the opening chords, we fall silent, listening, drinking in the music as it sinks and swells inside the car. I think of King David, baffled that he can please the Lord despite his fall from grace, baffled that the love of God reaches his broken soul. I think of Samson, blind and disgraced but strong again, pulling down the arches in a last heroic act.

I think, too, about love. We use the same word for such widely disparate and often conflicting emotions and actions. We grow up talking about our "God of love," and then we experience the tawdriness of human love, and somehow God falls in our eyes. Our anthems of praise fall flat because we do not believe them anymore, because in our failures we cannot raise our eyes to find the divine. We lose confidence in our ability to please God. Then, as we look to the ground, our shoulders hunched and our hearts broken with the effort of trying and failing, we mumble our own version of "hallelujah." Perhaps it is a simple prayer of sorrow or a finally genuine plea for help. Perhaps it's a kind act toward some other damned soul crouched far from the victory arch.

And then, in the depths, we feel it. Somehow our "cold and broken hallelujah" stumbled up to heaven. God's voice reached down to meet it, and the resulting chord begins to grow. The heart still stained and tattered by our attempts to find love here on earth gathers strength, and hope swells a "hallelujah" finally acceptable to a God who loves us despite our failures. Perhaps God loves us because when our failures broke us, we still tried to sing.

Some People Collect Spoons or Goofy Figurines
(May 2013)

I have little interest in decorative spoons, or stamps, or cheap porcelain angels. I like snow globes, but I would rather not have to dust them. Instead, I keep a collection of quotes. I collect quotes from books and talks, from random radio broadcasts or signs on museum walls. Some of the words inspire me. Some make me laugh. Some just sound nice rolling off my tongue. Because one cannot collect anything without imposing that collection on others, here are just a few of my quotes of the moment.

My Friend Ansel on ~~Love Friendship Art~~ Nature

Ansel Adams tops my list of quotes this week. In a letter to his best friend, Cedric Wright, he once wrote:

"I saw a big thundercloud move down over Half Dome, and it was so big and clear and brilliant that it made me see many things that were drifting around inside of me; things that related to those who are loved and those who are real friends."

Adams went on to describe his epiphanies about love, friendship and art. I intended to include those epiphanies here, but then I read this sentence at the end of the letter: "I wish the thundercloud had moved up over Tahoe and let loose on you; I could wish you nothing finer."

I thought of a long ago moonrise over the mountains that illuminated something both essential and inexplicable for me, and I remembered the profound peace of a certain slant of light drifting through the leaves on a quiet Sunday afternoon. I understand the power of nature to bring clarity and make of life something noble and grand and positively divine, if only for a fleeting moment.

Peter Lake on the Satisfaction of Responsibility

I love the book *Winter's Tale*, by Mark Helprin. For me, he is an Ansel Adams of words. In *Winter's Tale*, Helprin gives us the wonderful character of Peter Lake, a poet thief and master mechanic. Peter falls in love with Beverly, and at one point tells Beverly's father:

> *"When we drove across the lake this afternoon and Beverly held the little girl in her arms, I felt a responsibility far more satisfying than any pleasure I have ever known."*

While perhaps not the most evocative example of Helprin prose, that quote strikes a particular chord with me today, on the heels of Mother's Day. No satisfaction I have yet experienced compares with the glorious weight of another soul intertwined with mine.

Alice Ann on Teaching Teenagers

This week brings to a close another year of teaching early morning seminary to a group of bleary-eyed, yet wonderful teenagers. Each schoolday morning we gather at 6:00 a.m. and study scriptures together. Sometimes they sleep or do homework. Often they sing spontaneously and out of tune in the middle of a lesson, and even more often they wander hopelessly off topic. Sometimes they grumble about early mornings and other injustices, and sometimes they sit rather sullen in the shadow of their hoodies. I regularly despair of teaching them anything of value. And yet, as my friend Alice Ann Harrop reminded us in a recent teacher training workshop:

> *"The Spirit isn't stopped by hoodies."*

Despite the hoodies and the grumbling and the meanderings, I love these kids. I see glimmers of brilliance and compassion and deep thought that give me hope for the future.

Places and Seasons

Gems of the Heartland

(October 2010)

I had a lovely lunch last week at a café whimsically called "Incredibly Delicious," in the Aristocracy Hill district of downtown. While I must say that "hill" represents a bit of false advertising, the restaurant certainly earns its name. Café tables fill various rooms of a vintage house, and patrons choose from a small menu that changes daily. I ordered a spinach quiche and washed it down with Perrier, because any lunch that includes goat cheese cannot also include Sprite. Tasty as it was, the lunch primarily provided a landing spot for the pastry that followed. If I knew anything useful about baking, I would gush intelligently about the flourless chocolate torte and the "strawberry jobbie" (as my father-in-law called the impossibly light, vanilla strawberry cake). In lieu of intelligent gushing, I will simply say the pastries are divine and worth the short drive downtown.

Sitting in the restaurant, gazing at the art around me and the gardens outside, I began to ponder this town I find myself growing to love. We did not move from Vermont to the Heartland for the scenery, and at first (or second) glance the area has little to offer other than Target and corn. Over the past year, however, I have begun to discover a number of gems behind the fields and strip malls.

Even early on I learned the sheer joy of riding a bicycle along flat Midwestern farm roads with endless horizons. Swarms of birds erupt out of the fields or off the sparkling lake as I pass, swooping en masse from tree to lawn to rooftop. In the fall, thousands of geese hold convention across the street in the freshly harvested field, and their honking carries me home from blocks away. High above the gulls and geese, the hawks circle, occasionally coasting down to stand sentinel on a street lamp. I have always wanted to glimpse a hawk's view of my world.

Following family tradition, shortly after Thanksgiving we took Kristina to her first live performance of *The Nutcracker*. I expected a charming, but amateur, production of a favorite story. The Springfield Ballet Company and its alumni dancers delivered a performance and set that far exceeded my expectations, a perfect kickoff to the Christmas season.

Several months later, I attended the Muni, a local summer theater, to see their production of *Jesus Christ, Superstar*. Once again, I foolishly expected a slightly awkward amateur production. Once again, the local art scene smashed my expectations. Jesus, Judas, and Mary delivered topnotch performances, complemented by a talented supporting cast and crew.

In addition to culture, the cityscape itself offers charm, from stately, tree-lined boulevards to a magnificent capitol dome to the flawless artistry of Frank Lloyd Wright and his Dana-Thomas House.

Closer to home, my daughter has chosen her favorite local spots. The Viennese carousel at the mall was an early magical discovery, and Kristina frequently begs to "ride the ponies." In addition, once each week or so we spend an afternoon at the local public library, which boasts a fabulous children's area and even a Barnes and Noble style café and bookstore. For two dollars I can happily feed both my sugar and my book addictions. Who could possibly ask for more?

Wherever we go, here in the Heartland, I have been struck by the sheer friendliness of the people. I cannot remember passing by a single store clerk, be it the shelf-stocker at the grocery store or the restaurant server with the intriguing tattoos, who failed to smile genuinely and say "hello" as if they were truly happy to see me. Warm welcomes extend far beyond the shop aisle here. Our movers brought Midwestern friendship to New England with the moving van and have remained good friends, introducing us to auctions and mostly delicious experimental barbecues. Their friendship was just the first in a line of unexpectedly delightful relationships.

I have no idea where the next five years will find me or what adventures await our family. Right now, on this sunny autumn afternoon, I am happily a Midwestern woman.

Aromatherapy

(November 2010)

I walked outside just now and took a deep breath as I contemplated the next two and a half hours of solitude. In the air I caught a faint scent of new rain. I closed my eyes and inhaled again, more deeply this time, searching. Depending on the season, the musky scent of rain beginning to fall takes me one of two places.

A chilly rain, like today, takes me to Logan Canyon in early autumn. I have left the car at the parking lot at Third Dam and found a trail heading...upward. It does not really matter where the trail leads. I hike quickly but aimlessly, the chill giving me energy and the mist over the mountains shrouding any pretended goal. I revel in the solitude of mist and twirling leaves, the drip of the rain and the scent of the earth.

A warm rain, on the other hand, sends me to the desert in the midst of a downpour in Mesa, Arizona. As usual, given the rarity of a rainstorm here, I have left the windows down on my parents' Ford Courier truck. I run out into the rain, laughing, to close them. I toss a towel on the seat for the ride home, but tomorrow's blistering heat will dry the upholstery just fine. The rain covers the hubcaps, and we splash in the street, shirts now a second skin and hair drenched.

I love the power of smell to unlock memories, transporting me to almost forgotten moments in times and places I have not visited in years. A trip to the grocery store leaves me paused in the coffee aisle, my body in County Market but my head far away in Alaska. At 4 a.m. we have gallons of coffee waiting. The sun rose long ago, and the vacationing fishermen begin to trickle into the dining room. Randy has the float planes waiting at the beach, and the guides swallow their last bites of bacon and eggs. A few hours of folding clothes or cleaning rooms will earn me an afternoon to explore the tundra.

Far from the wilderness of the Alaskan bush, I find myself strangely enamored with the smell of diesel fumes on a passing city bus. Nasty smell, I suppose, but for me it smells of freedom and adventure, of early morning in Chicago. For the moment, I am fifteen, traveling cross country alone. Just after dawn, we near the Greyhound station. I gaze up at the skyscrapers, smile at the busy and unfamiliar din of horns honking. In another 24 hours, I will yearn for a long shower and a quiet bed, but here in the city the tingle of adventure quickens my step. I want to dance about, but instead I stroll through the bus terminal in my best imitation of a seasoned traveler.

Back in the Midwest again, but much older, I search for Christmas candles. I find it difficult to choose among the pine of childhood Christmas trees, the vanilla that reminds me of the eggnog at Mrs. Gleich's annual Christmas bazaar, or the spicy citrus of the oranges we used to cover in cloves and tuck away in our sock drawers. Perhaps I should simply buy them all and bring decades of Christmases together in a whiff.

Backward Glancing
(June 2011)

The upcoming weekend finds me traveling back to Vermont for the first time since we moved to the Midwest two years ago. My somewhat nomadic lifestyle left me in Vermont far longer than any other place I have called "home" over the years. I left readily; Lot's wife and I have little in common. And yet, the thought of New England air sends me looking back fondly.

I picture rolling green hills and lakes clean enough for swimming. I feel the magnetic pull of the stretch of meadow at Fays Corner in Richmond and the early morning mist over Lake Champlain. My feet itch for a walk along Burlington's Church Street, past the usual crowd of 21st century New England hippies. We will have just missed the Jazz Festival on the waterfront, but perhaps we can stop by the Ben & Jerry's scoop shop for a double scoop of Chocolate Fudge Brownie and Cherry Garcia (frozen yogurt if I feel like being healthy, ice cream if I feel like walking on the wild side).

I find myself picturing favorite spots with layers of memories. For instance, I remember shopping on Church Street 25 years ago. I was a young college student, playing my way through the summer as the maître d' at a country inn on North Hero Island. With a day off and my roommate's car, I drove in to Burlington to soak up the summer crowds along the cobblestone street of the marketplace.

Seven years later, I returned to Church Street. I bypassed What Ale's You and the Skirack this time in favor of street vendors and the Discovery Channel Store. Along with my two-year-old son, I embraced life with gusto. Devin turned heads with his blond curls, his movie star sunglasses, and a heart-stopping smile. We paused to climb every boulder between the Unitarian Church at the head of Church Street to Sweetwater's Restaurant near the bottom.

Over the next eighteen years, we returned to the cobblestones on frigid New Year's Eves for the annual First Night Dancing Dragons Parade, on humid summer afternoons for Italian sausage from Bookie's street cart, and occasionally for sumptuous desserts at Leunig's Bistro.

I miss the feel of Vermont, from the taste of the air on the first full-blown summer day in June to the unapologetically tree-hugging politics. I miss the bluntness of native Vermonters (although one has to search harder and harder to find them these days) and the eccentricities of my fellow church members there. I miss the music, from Mozart on the shores of Lake Champlain to the hot summer day we spent at the Vermont Reggae Festival in a rolling meadow up north. I dream of a day beginning on the Sunset Ridge trail on Mount Mansfield and ending in the charm of a tiny theatre in Waitsfield.

July will find me once again contentedly roaring past endless cornfields on the motorcycle and anticipating the glory of Friday night football underneath the lights. For this slice of early summer, however, my heart returns to an earlier home.

St. Louis Celebration

(January 2013)

Just about 19 years ago, Brad and I drove to Washington, D.C. (or, more accurately, the LDS temple in Kensington, Maryland) to celebrate our marriage with our families and some close friends. We have all added a few wrinkles since that January day. We have also added a few children, a few addresses, a few jobs, a dog, hundreds of sunrises and sunsets, a little rain, and a few spectacular storms.

In honor of all those years of more sunshine than storm, Brad and I decided to run away to St. Louis for the day. After all, we have lived in central Illinois for nearly four years now, and we have never explored what turns out to be a surprisingly charming city. The weather gods blessed us with a January thaw and sun. Consequently, after waving the kids off to school, we jumped into the car and headed south.

We intended to start our adventure at the Butterfly House in Chesterfield but arrived to find the site closed for the month. Feeling quite mellow and adaptable, we shrugged our shoulders, took a picture of a huge stone butterfly, and moved on to downtown St. Louis.

Next stop: the Cathedral Basilica of Saint Louis, with 83,000 square feet of mosaic art created by twenty artists out of 41.5 million tesserae. (Yeah, I had to look that one up. Tesserae are the little squares of stone or glass that go into a mosaic.) Mosaic covers every bit of the massive ceilings and much of the walls, depicting Biblical scenes in the rich tones of over 8000 colors. The beauty of the scene certainly inspires awe, if not worship.

And awe inspires...hunger, apparently. Fortunately, the Cathedral Basilica lies in the heart of the upscale Central West End, close to the trendy restaurants and shops of Euclid Avenue. Hoping to infuse a bit of health into our day of play, we stopped in at OR Smoothie and Café for a lunch of organic, vegan yumminess, topped off with a couple of signature smoothies. I confess to stopping for a chocolate filled croissant when our after lunch stroll took us past the St. Louis Bread Company, but the guilt feelings faded quickly as the chocolate oozed over my fingers.

Pleasantly full, we turned our attention to nearby Forest Park. As we wound our way through the park, we stopped first at the Jewel Box, a charming Art Deco floral conservancy characterized by its unique cantilevered glass walls. The greenhouse is a popular wedding spot, and even without the colorful gardens that surround the building in warmer seasons, it offers a lovely retreat from city life. We had the flowers to ourselves for a few minutes, and we drank in the rich air of the lush indoor garden.

After a few turns of the park road, we passed by the St. Louis Zoo (packed with families enjoying a rare warm day in January) and drove up to the St. Louis Art Museum. Through the feature exhibit, we watched the evolution of the masterpieces of Federico Barocci, then wandered through galleries of Impressionist, Realist, Asian and African art. I finally learned why in the world so many talented artists waste their time painting fruit, and I stood nose to nose with one of Degas' dancers. (The girl had an attitude! My kind of girl...) I even discovered a new addition to my list of favorite paintings: John Martin's "Sadak in Search of the Waters of Oblivion." Art does good things for the soul.

We wound down with a little window shopping in Richmond Heights and stuffed ourselves with a late dinner at Maggianos Little Italy. Good conversation carried us home, and I crawled happily into bed just after midnight. What a glorious day!

The Surprise Love Affair Continues
(June 2013)

I never expected to like St. Louis. News reports of kidnappings and other crimes over the years left me with a sour opinion only enhanced by the rather large footprint of Anheuser-Busch and billboards advertising the likes of Hustler's Boutique Erotica. Nothing screams "redneck" quite like American beer and Larry Flint.

After a couple of years of monthly jaunts down to the LDS temple in St. Louis, I discovered Trader Joe's and Sweet Tomatoes, and my perspective slowly began to shift. After all, who can resist TJ's Cookie Butter or Sweet Tomatoes' won ton chicken salad with one of those delicious blueberry muffins on the side?

But the love affair truly began last January, when Brad and I finally made our first recreational visit to St. Louis. (Yes, it took us nearly four years to make the trip.) We took the kids back for spring break playtime at the fabulous City Museum, and a dear friend fed my cultural habit with a lovely evening at Spring to Dance 2013. Consequently, when we found ourselves with a rare opportunity to sneak away for a quick overnight trip without the kiddos, Brad and I once again made our way south.

We started on Thursday evening with Twangfest. You probably know exactly what to expect from an event called "Twangfest." I did not. I vaguely expected something on the order of bluegrass or the country music of my parents' generation. While Conway Twitty would have suited me just fine, I found myself pleasantly surprised with the range of sound and styles offered through the course of an evening at Blueberry Hill. Scarlet Tanager, Shivering Timbers, and Motel Mirrors opened with an eclectic offering of indie pop and country, alternatively haunting and playful vocals, fabulous harmonies and some killer string bass. Joe Pug headlined, and to be honest, we left after a few songs. Joe channels Bob Dylan just fine, but after the color and depth of the previous bands, he lacked oomph.

We crashed at a hotel in Clayton for the night and made our way back to the Delmar Loop area the next day for an afternoon of discovery. After a walk down memory lane at Vintage Vinyl, a bit of incense at one of the fair trade boutiques and a few photo ops with the artsy Loop manikins and Chuck Berry (or at least his likeness), we dined sumptuously on Syrian food at Ranoush. The restaurant had me at the hummus and sealed the deal with stuffed grape leaves, baba ganoush (which I would order even if it weren't delicious, simply because the name sounds so nice rolling off my tongue), mint tea and knafeh, among other delights.

Pleasantly full, we rounded off our afternoon browsing through the wonderful Componere Gallery of Art, chatting with owner and artist Eleanor Ruder and falling in love with sculptures by Alexzine Lewis and the copper and aluminum trees of Omer Huremovic.

After a requisite stop at Trader Joe's for Dark Chocolate Almond Toffee (yes, you must try it), we made our way home to continue the love affair another day.

A Perfect Day

(May 2014)

Every so often, on rare and memorable occasions, life hands out perfect days. These are days to savor, days that leave an imprint on our souls. I experienced the gift of one such day recently. A number of years ago, two dear friends and I hatched up a Mothers' Day plan while pushing baby joggers up steep Vermont hills on our ritual morning walk. What better way to celebrate motherhood, we posited, than by escaping responsibility for a day? So we ran away to Montreal for Mothers' Day weekend, returning for Sunday's bounty of cards and hugs and food cooked by hands other than our own.

When I left the Vermont hills for Midwestern cornfields, I brought the tradition with me and have sporadically lassoed various friends into my annual escape. This year, Mothers' Day Saturday dawned brilliantly sunny and pleasantly warm. Four of us passed the two-hour drive to St. Louis switching comfortably between the trivial and the profound with ease born of long friendship and shared experience.

We stopped first at the St. Louis Art Museum (SLAM), drawn by the traveling exhibit: Impressionist France. Through the lens of Charles Marville and the brushes of Claude Monet, Jean-Francois Millet, Edouard Manet and their compatriots, we toured Paris and the French countryside, 19th century factories and the coastline. The washerwomen of Jules Breton struck a particular chord, goddesses in bare feet and white caps.

Leaving the stately columns of SLAM, we headed to 39th Street and Sweet Art, a neighborhood café, bakeshop and art studio owned by baker Reine Bayoc and her artist husband Cbabi Bayoc. While indulging in vegan eats and not quite so vegan but oh so amazing pastries, we discovered Cbabi's "365 Days with Dad," a project of 365 paintings celebrating black fatherhood. His paintings are worlds apart from Jules Breton but equally powerful in their own sphere.

Still munching vegan brownies, salted caramel bars and hummingbird cake, we made our way downtown to a fantastic production of Joseph and the Amazing Technicolor Dreamcoat. Joseph and his brothers delivered, as did the opulent Fox Theater.

Once back in the sunshine, we wandered for a time, drunk on summery air and the wonder of a few hours without schedules and demands. We stopped first at St. Francis Xavier College Church, pausing to meditate in the hush of intricate stained glass and worshippers waiting for their turn at confession. Around the corner, on the campus of Saint Louis University, we found a delightful collection of sculptures, a perfect picnic spot tucked among perennials, and a couple of stately stone lions watching over the Moolah Temple.

We rounded out our adventure under the tutelage of Mai Truong, the chatty founder of the OR Smoothie & Café in the Central West End. Sipping power smoothies and munching Vietnamese spring rolls, we reflected on a glorious day in the middle of lives that, for all of their twists and turns, have treated us remarkably well.

My grandfather loved the song "A Perfect Day," by Carrie Jacobs-Bond. "When you come to the end of a perfect day," she wrote, "and you sit alone with your thought, ...mem'ry has painted this perfect day with colors that never fade, and we find at the end of a perfect day the soul of a friend we've made." Ms. Jacobs-Bond wrote those lyrics 100 years ago after watching a magnificent sunset at the close of a glorious day spent motoring with friends. I think perhaps I know just what she was thinking that evening.

Late Summer Reflections

(August 2014)

An errand took me into WalMart the other day, and I noticed with surprise the rows and rows of binders and crayons, pencils and spiral notebooks. I flipped through my mental calendar and realized with a shock that my children start school in just nine days. Decades ago, I measured the end game of summertime by the progress of back-to-school sewing. Sometime around midsummer, Mother would take us downtown to the fabric store and let us pick out patterns and fabric for our new school clothes. (Fifth grade included a particularly nifty pair of gouchos, light blue denim with a matching shirt. Oh, but I felt stunning!) After a trip to the laundromat and some time spent pulling the fabric to line up the grain, out came the patterns and the interfacing and the black Singer sewing machine. Many seams and zippers later, the fabric began to look like a wardrobe. And in the last days before school, Mother hemmed and added the finishing touches. I eagerly planned my back-to-school outfit, counting down the days.

Somehow, I failed to catch the sewing bug myself, and without the whir of that ancient Singer, summertime meanders along at its own pace, leaving me rather shocked to find myself at the end of the ride, not quite prepared for autumn and falling far short of the lofty goals I set for myself ten weeks ago. The biography I started writing in 2011 remains just short of complete. My blog suffers from neglect. I half-read several books and completed none of them. I never ran that 10K I intended to run this summer.

However, while the writing fell by the wayside (again), we built good memories. I watched while Son #1 married a wonderful woman, and I smiled at the delight of Son #3 as he hiked with me along the edge of a mountainside. I ran dozens of miles and biked hundreds more, clearing my head and finding my endurance. I dated my husband and discovered downtown Springfield with my daughter. I even enjoyed the state fair for once, despite the rain that soaked us while we screamed and laughed on the rides.

The next few days will find me wandering those school supply aisles with a list in my hand and an excited third grader by my side. Perhaps on my way out of the store I will casually drop my list of summer goals in the garbage can and start fresh for autumn, buoyed up by good memories and the warmth of summer on the wane.

Football Weather

(September 2010)

In the early years of our marriage, autumn began each year with my husband's wistful pronouncement, "This is football weather." Brad played high school and semi-pro football and kept warm memories of those days. While I never played football, I love the unique energy that comes with early autumn, the combination of ripeness and new beginnings that follows the delicious sluggishness of August.

Today was, indeed, a football day in all its Midwestern glory. Bright sunshine in a virtually cloudless sky teased the sweatshirt off my daughter's shoulders by the second quarter of this morning's high school game. The wind set the cornfields whispering along our drive home. This phenomenon of brown corn standing in the field for weeks puzzled me at first after years among the sweet corn fields in New England. By now, I have begun to tell the passing seasons by the height and color of the corn.

On my husband's insistence, I donned helmet and jacket this afternoon with the promise to take the motorcycle for a long ride while he cleaned the house. (How could I not acquiesce to such a demand?) For two hours I rode past fields and silos, sleepy towns and peaceful cemeteries. With the roar of the bike to keep the world at bay, I let my thoughts wander and relaxed into the rhythm of the back roads. Chilled by the wind, I returned home to my first hot chocolate of the season, a hot bath, and a book. Hooray for football weather!

Autumn Snapshots

(September 2010)

My friend Judy Gile always said that foliage season in Vermont peaked on October 9, and Vermont generally complied with her wishes. Judy had that effect on the world around her. From our home in Sherwood Forest, not far from Burlington and Lake Champlain, we claimed a view of Camel's Hump and the hills and valleys of hardwood forests leading up to it. I particularly loved to gaze down over the town to see the mist rising above the river and the Round Church gleaming stark white against a backdrop of orange, wine, and the occasional splash of red. Closer to home, the trees along our road formed a yellow canopy over our frosty morning jaunt to the bus stop.

On Saturday mornings, we walked through the covered bridge to the football field. Mt. Mansfield presided in the distance, brilliant foliage lined the river, and the clang of the cowbell signalled each Wolverine touchdown. Later in the season, we kicked the snow at our feet and huddled under blankets while we cheered. The anticipation of hot chocolate by the wood stove kept us warm on the inside, at least.

In addition to football, we are also a Macintosh family. Every year I had to remind myself to wait past first frost for the Macs to grow red and sweet. Then, on a sunny Saturday morning, we rambled through the orchard with our wagon, brown bags full of drops for applesauce and half bushel bags for smooth pie apples. The scent of fresh cider donuts eventually pulled us out of the trees. Then we piled in the car, apples at our feet and crumbs on our smiling lips, anticipating the first pie of the season.

I miss New England autumns, bursting as they are with homebaked coziness and the tingle of promise. However, though I love first snows, I do not miss the long winter that follows. Those Vermont winters made the move to the belly of the country a little easier. Few people travel to central Illinois for the lush scenery. Still, a misty autumn morning holds promise with or without hills rolling with color. The huge harvesters lumber down the farm road outside my kitchen window, reminding me that my horizon now filled with fields of brown corn will transform overnight.

That right there is what I love about autumn. No New Year's resolutions for me. In the dead of winter, I would rather curl up next to the fire and read. But autumn...now that is the time for change. I send the kids back to school, dizzy with the possibilities before me. Then I open my journal, watch out the window as my horizon expands before my eyes, and plan my dreams into focus.

Christmas Moments

(December 2010)

During every pledge drive, NPR listeners take to the airwaves to recount their "driveway moments," those times when an intriguing story keeps them glued to the radio in a parked car just outside their own front door. Likewise, we laugh at ourselves about "Hallmark moments" that find us secretly brushing away a tear in the card aisle or choking up while watching a T-Mobile commercial.

Yesterday I had yet another in a series of "Christmas moments" that have made the season surprisingly joyful for me this year. I have no particular problem with Christmas, no painful memories or existential crises, but I do tend to let the materialism and general holiday stress wear me down. Yesterday afternoon I held my sleeping daughter in my arms next to a tiny Christmas tree and drifted off to the sounds of the Salt Lake Children's Choir singing carols. I think the angelic host must have included some children in the chorus when they sang to the shepherds.

Kristina and I had spent the morning with her preschool class on a Bethlehem journey at a local church. Searching for the Christ Child, we followed the Magi to Herod's palace and the home of Elizabeth and

Zacharias, through a shepherd's field where the sheep huddled against a prairie wind, and to a crowded inn. Finally we presented gifts of wooden stars to the Child as he slept in his mother's arms next to Joseph, who soothed a nervous donkey in the neighboring stall. Cold wind seeped through the stable walls, and Baby Jesus was, after all, just a doll, but the children stood entranced at the manger. I nearly cried as I walked through the nearby marketplace, past child actors asking "Did you find Him?" with a light in their eyes.

Early in the season, I shared another Christmas moment with my teenage son as we attended Rochester High School's annual Madrigal Tea. The choral department transformed the auditorium and took us back through the centuries with flute and jesters and music that settled on my soul like starlight. Music always stirs me, but Christmas music with candles and the warmth of good friends touches my heart with particular poignancy.

The following week, we forced our reluctant boys into dress shirts, braved the first real cold of the season and entered the magical world of *The Nutcracker*. Kristina's eyes lit up when she saw her dance teacher on stage and watched Drosselmeyer's magic. I remembered back fondly to my own ballet years, when dancing in *The Nutcracker* ushered in the Christmas season for me, and I love that my children allow me to impose my past on their present.

Some of my favorite Christmas moments pass quietly in the evening, with the house dark except for the lights on the tree and in the windows of the village above our fireplace. Brad and I chat about inconsequential happenings of the day and mostly just relax into the best of the Christmas season.

Happily, I find myself this December in the midst of some in depth spiritual study. I discovered some weeks ago that with a little more intense reading, I could finish James Talmage's *Jesus the Christ* on Christmas Eve. Thus, the Advent has me immersed in the life of the Savior whose birth we celebrate. As I read of His miracles and His teachings, and as I become more aware of His hand in the minutia of my life, my love for the Savior deepens, and my journey to Bethlehem and the gardens of Gethsemane and the resurrection finds color and music like never before.

Creative Writing

Martha's Memory

(Historical Fiction – April 2015)

It is spring again. In years past, I would fill my days watching over the barley harvest and preparing for our Passover feast. This afternoon, I sit by the window as a gentle rain washes over my small garden. When the sun returns tomorrow, I will harvest the peas and tend to the grape vines and fig trees that grace the far corner. Today, I listen to the rain and gaze out over the valley. A mother carries her son past my window, singing softly to him as she makes her way to market.

A memory tickles the back of my mind, and I see myself on that same road, skipping to market hand in hand with a chortling toddler. Mother had matzah to make for the Passover. The house smelled of warm bread, and Lazarus was in fine form already, snatching piles of dough and reaching his chubby hands too close to the fire. Mother laughed and pushed us outdoors. "Off you go," she said. Try as we might, none of us could find it in our hearts to lecture the laughing boy. With his infectious grin and ready hugs, Lazarus simply left joy in his wake. And so we skipped off down the road to look at the lambs waiting to be purchased for the feast. They bleated behind the gate, oblivious to their starring role in the events of the week.

While Lazarus played with the lambs, I sat on a rock, feeling the sun warm my cheeks. I sensed movement to my left and opened my eyes to see a boy duck around the corner of the enclosure. I knew everyone in Bethany, but this was a stranger, a tall, lanky boy wearing a traveling cloak. Though I lived within walking distance of Jerusalem, we rarely ventured far from our village. Particularly during feast time, Mother worried for our safety among the strangers in the city. I longed to know about far-off Egypt, Rome or Greece. Even Hebron or Galilee sounded exotic to my eleven- year old imagination.

"Where do you come from?" I called, a little surprised at my own boldness.

A face peered around the corner of the stall. Dark eyes sparkled over a sharp nose, and a thin hand pushed a strand of black hair back from the face of a boy probably two years older than I. He seemed pleased to have someone to talk with.

"You looked so peaceful, with your face turned up to the sun," he said. "I did not wish to frighten you."

Truthfully, the boy had startled me, but my desire to hear about his travels overcame any shyness. "You look as if you have traveled some distance," I said. "Where do you call home?"

"Father and I came from Kerioth for the Passover. He has business with friends in the village tonight, but tomorrow we go to Jerusalem."

I handed the boy a bit of bread, and we chewed in silence for a while, listening to the bleating of the lambs and watching Lazarus throw pebbles into the ditch.

"I love the city during feast time," the boy reflected, almost to himself.

"I have never seen Jerusalem during Passover, actually," I admitted. "Mother and Father worry about all of the people. Or maybe they are afraid I will sneak off with a caravan. What is it like?"

The boy proceeded to tell me about the markets, the people from as far away as Ethiopia. He described the noise of the doves in the courtyard of the temple, waiting to be sacrificed. Inns were crowded with pilgrims and merchants. Tradesmen like his father made more profit during Passover than at any other time of the year. My own father had told me about the crowds in the city, of course, but as the boy talked, the music and the prayers, the smells of exotic food and the cries of the beggars came alive. I closed my eyes to imagine the scene.

"You love it, do you not?" I said. It was not a question, really. I could tell by his voice that he could hardly wait to enter the city again. "Tell me your favorite part. Tell me a story."

The look on his face changed. I worried for a minute that I had said something wrong, but then he spoke quietly, almost reverently. "It was last year," he began. "It was my first trip to Jerusalem, and Father took me to the temple just before we left town with the other merchants. I listened to the men discussing scripture, arguing about laws and prophecies, comparing the notes of the famous rabbis. I was surprised to see a boy among the men. He was about my age, but when he spoke, the men nodded as if he had said something wise. I walked closer, standing just on the edge of the crowd. An old man, clearly a respected teacher, asked the boy a question. I do not even remember the question or the answer, but I remember the boy's voice. His voice was not particularly deep, nor did he speak loudly. But somehow, when he spoke, I just had to listen. He knew what he was saying was true, without apology, without doubt. I study the prophecies a great deal, and my father says I know more than most of the men in our synagogue, but this boy…when he spoke, it was as if the prophet Isaiah himself stood in front of me. Suddenly, I understood things I never even imagined before."

The traveler stopped there, as if embarrassed about his excitement. "Did you speak to him?" I asked.

"No. I just stood there. I was too amazed to open my mouth. But he looked up once, looked straight at me. His eyes were as old as Abraham, and I thought maybe he could see right into my thoughts. He gave a little nod, as if he knew me, as if he knew something in my heart that even I did not know. Then it was time to leave. I will never forget that. I keep thinking someday I will see him again, and I think of all the questions I want to ask."

Just then, Lazarus threw his arms around my neck, and the spell was broken. The boy stood up, brushing crumbs off his cloak. "I should get back to the market," he said. "Father will wonder where I have run off to." And with that, he was gone.

I have thought many times over the years about that afternoon. I do not often call out to strangers, and I realized after he left that I never even asked his name, but the look on his face as he told of his experience in the temple stuck with me. Never in my wildest imaginings did I dream that one day I would once again meet not only the boy from Kerioth but also the remarkable boy from the temple.

Years later, Lazarus ran into my garden one afternoon, his face alive with the excitement of discovery. He was still my laughing boy, but older now, with a young family of his own. "Martha," he panted. "Come with me. The grapes can wait, but this cannot!"

Years had passed, but I had never learned to resist the enthusiasm of my favorite brother. I washed my hands in the fountain and followed him to the hillside. A crowd had gathered there, and a man sat in their midst, teaching. He spoke of ordinary things, of planting and harvesting, grains and birds. But the ordinary took on new meaning for me that day. I stood toward the back for a time, but before long I joined Lazarus and our sister Mary at the man's feet. He challenged us to love even our enemies, and as I sat there in the spell of his voice, I thought I could love even the Romans if he asked me to. He spoke simply, with a power greater than his voice, greater than the words themselves or the challenge they presented. He spoke with authority and with love, with an immense love that I felt envelop all of us on that hillside.

As he spoke, I noticed his companions nearby, sitting in groups of two or three and asking questions from time to time. One man in particular caught my eye. He seemed familiar, like a face from a long distant memory. I thought perhaps he had visited with my father in his shop or worked in the fields during harvest, although his thin hands were not the hands of a laborer. He, too, listened intently to the teacher, pushing his fingers through his black hair from time to time when a point of the discussion particularly engaged him. I had almost located him in my memory when the discussion came to a close and Mary's voice at my side interrupted my thoughts.

"Jesus," she said. "We would be honored if you and your friends would take a meal with us."

The teacher looked at us then and smiled. That evening was the first of many that he dined with us, sometimes in the company of his disciples and sometimes on his own, a weary traveler seeking quiet refuge from the crowds that always seemed to follow him. In time, I remembered his companion as the Passover traveler of my youthful memory. Once, I heard him retell the story of the boy in the temple. Jesus watched him quietly as he spoke, his eyes almost sad. "Judas," he asked. "Have you found what you were seeking?" Neither man spoke for a minute, and soon the conversation turned to other topics.

For some reason, I never told Judas that I remembered him. If he ever connected me with the young girl of Bethany and her laughing baby brother, he never mentioned it. I had many occasions to see him over the next couple of years, and I began to understand the sadness in Jesus' eyes as he listened to Judas speak. The sparkle in the eyes and the fire of testimony that had so animated Judas in the beginning began to fade over time. He moved more and more away from the group discussions, preferring to occupy his hours with the administrative affairs of the disciples. Once a dynamic speaker who could capture an audience with his fervor and intellect, he gradually spoke less and less and seemed troubled when Jesus began to talk openly about his calling as the Messiah. Occasionally, I would see Jesus and Judas walking on the hillside together, talking earnestly.

The last time I saw Judas was in Bethany, just days before the awful Friday of the crucifixion. I served dinner and listened as the men spoke. There was a heaviness in the air, like the gloom before a thunderstorm. Jesus himself seemed grieved by a silent sorrow, and he taught with more intensity, as if anxious that we would remember every word. We did not understand when he spoke of his own death, not until later. But we felt his love, and we, too, grieved, without understanding why. As dinner closed, Mary entered the room, weeping. She approached Jesus, and he nodded, almost imperceptibly. She brought out a container of spikenard and worked it gently into his feet, massaging each callous. As she worked quietly, Judas spoke up from the corner of the room.

"How can you allow this, Jesus? Surely it would be better to sell that precious ointment and use the money for the poor?" His eyes, as he looked scornfully at my sister, had finally lost the last vestige of wonder that sparkled in them when we first met. Jesus rebuked him gently, but firmly. He had lessons still to teach us, and Judas had his own part to play in the drama that unfolded over the next week.

Death Awaiting Ephiphany
(December 2012)

I avoid looking on death,

Averting my gaze and holding my breath

As I pedal past the raccoon, spread-eagle on the road,

Its innards outside,

A bewildered expression frozen on the bandit face

(or is it decomposition that makes the eyes so sad?).

Once I dressed a friend for burial,

A gathering of women tugging underclothes over a limp body,

Wiping body fluids that escaped out of the eye socket,

Rust-colored tears.

We laughed over shared memories,

Philosophized about resurrection and heaven,

as one must while handling the dead.

It was years before I could eat barbecue sauce

Without picturing those tears dripping toward a cold metal gurney,

A vision of death not quite ready for company.

I suppose decay, rather than death, repulses me

(or frightens?),

The unnatural tilt of a powerless neck,

An inner life left in disarray,

Rotting in the glare of an oblivious sun.

Body bereft of spirit,

Untidy emotion awaiting epiphany.

Made in the USA
Middletown, DE
27 March 2022

63236397R00089